Primroses and Polyanthus

MODERN PRIMROSE HYBRIDS

Primroses and Polyanthus

ROY GENDERS

and

H. C. TAYLOR

CRITERION BOOKS

New York

Printed in Great Britain

Foreword

Here, we believe, is the first book for at least fifty years on the quaint primroses and polyanthus of Tudor and modern times; plants which once again have become 'the fashion'. This revival of popularity may be somehow associated with the dawning of a new Elizabethan era, or it may be a response to articles, by the authors and others, that have appeared in the gardening press; it could be due to the fact that this is now an age of the small garden to which these lovely old-world plants are eminently suited. The cottage garden of Tudor days has its counterpart in the suburban garden of to-day, and over a period of nearly four hundred years the wheel has turned the full cycle. More than two hundred varieties in singles and doubles and the numerous quaint forms have been catalogued, many for the first time, the work having taken more than four years to accomplish. In this connection the authors owe a very great debt to Miss C. M. Chance for her long hours of research undertaken at the Lindley Library, for without her great assistance the chapters on double primroses would have been extremely difficult to write. We also extend our thanks to the Librarian and Staff of the Lindley Library and to the Editor of *Gardening Illustrated* for his kind permission to look through back numbers.

Our thanks are also due to Mr. James Laver, of the Victoria and Albert Museum in London, for his generous help in providing valuable information on sixteenth- and seventeenth-century costumes and on the origin of many of the old-fashioned primroses; as also to Mr. L. D. Hills for his valued suggestions on the

presentation of our material; and to Doris Gatling for the typing
and preparation of our manuscript from a large pile of notes.

CHARLES TAYLOR,
Glazeley Gardens,
Bridgnorth, Salop.

November, 1953

ROY GENDERS,
Hillway, Stepney Road,
Scarborough, Yorks.

Contents

Illustrations

11

CHAPTER I

The Return of the Primrose

Truly, one of the most significant happenings in the world of horticulture in this new Elizabethan era is the return to favour of the primrose and polyanthus. By this we mean the quaint old English primrose, esteemed in every garden, of both cottage and manor house, during the reign of the first Elizabeth. It was then the most truly English of all flowers; it must, in fact, have been a familiar April sight on our banks and in our hedgerows from the earliest days, for no other flower blooms to perfection in all parts of Great Britain, nor does any other flower represent the countryside of our childhood more completely than the familiar yellow primrose. We all know it, we have all gathered the delicately perfumed flowers in March, April and May, from the hedgerows of Sussex and the West Country, from the apple orchards of Hereford and Gloucestershire; from the dales of North Yorkshire and the Lake District; from the banks of those delightful Derbyshire streams, the Derwent, the Dove, and the Wye. Childhood jaunts, a rattling Ford car, baskets of mushrooms and blackberries in autumn, and primroses in spring; those are indeed reminders of happy days and of our pleasure in the two most exciting seasons of the year. Quaint and charming is the primrose of our land in its many different forms and varieties, which breathe the very essence of springtime, heralding days in the sun and the sound of bat and ball on playground and village green.

The earliest writers on horticulture all mentioned the primrose frequently and at length; indeed it was, with them, as popular a flower as are the lupin, dahlia and chrysanthemum with

modern growers, and as were the geranium, marguerite and helio-
trope with Victorian gardeners. During the sixteenth century
the flower enjoyed a considerable vogue, being much used in
designs for purses, pin-cushions, fire screens and embroidery in
diverse forms. The native primrose symbolized England more
appropriately than any other flower, and the English gave it the
prominence it deserved. We have evidence that one of the very
earliest writers, Tabernaemontanus, knew the double sulphur
primrose back in the year 1500, and the great Elizabethan John
Gerard, in his *Historie of Plants*, published in 1597, makes frequent
mention of the plant, and illustrates the double white. Knowing
the ability of the wild primrose to 'sport' in various forms, we are
entitled to suppose that the doubles, hose-in-hose and Jack-in-the-
Greens must all have been found growing under natural conditions in all parts of Britain; indeed their numbers must have been
legion, certain forms and colours possibly confining themselves to
certain districts. Indeed, in a letter to the editor of *The Field* of
August 1953, a correspondent tells us that they still abound in the
grounds of an ancient manor in Dorset. As travel was limited and
as gardening practice knew nothing akin to modern commerciali-
zation, there would be no widespread distribution of the plants in
Tudor times, but Parkinson, the authority of early Stuart days,
knew a number of diverse forms. In his famous *Paradisi*, published in 1629, he refers to the hose-in-hose, as reminding him of
'the breeches men do wear', one blossom arising out of another
and creating a most quaint appearance of one Tudor-style stocking in another. These hose of early days were knitted with a much
stiffer and stronger wool than we use to-day, and it was the custom
for one stocking to be placed inside another before being passed on
to the wearer. One may go further in the derivation of the term
'hose-in-hose', for, as Mr. James Laver has pointed out, a delightful picture, 'A Gentleman and a Lady at the Harpsichord', by
Gabrielle Metsu, in the possession of Lady Ludlow, plainly
shows the 'Gentleman' wearing double hose. One pair of stock-
ings reach to just below the knees, an inner pair to the thighs,
giving the effect of 'hose-*in*-hose'. This, too, is the primrose of
Mrs. Ewing's *Mary's Meadow*. Shakespeare frequently mentioned

the primrose and in *Hamlet*, written about the year 1600, he writes:

> *Himself the primrose path of dalliance treads.*

And in *A Winter's Tale*:

> *pale primroses*
> *That die unmarried ere they can behold*
> *Bright Phoebus in his strength.*

Again in *Cymbeline*:

> *Thou shalt not lack*
> *The flower that's like thy face, pale primrose.*

'Pale Primroses' is a phrase to which Shakespeare returns again and again. And Milton has

> *Soft silken Primrose fading timelesslie.*

In *The Two Noble Kinsmen*, Beaumont and Fletcher write of:

> *Primrose, first-born child of Ver,*
> *Merry Springtime's harbinger . . .*

The primrose was, of course, a part of England's landscape, as familiar to her cottage gardens as are now the rose and the daffodil.

The Jack-in-the-Greens, too, were extensively cultivated about the year 1600. Also known as Jack-in-the-Pulpit, these delightful plants are generally of the now familiar polyanthus habit, possessing long stems that make them an ideal cut-flower subject; and the bloom has a Tudor 'ruff' or row of green petals beneath the bloom. As they are easy to grow and increase, it is surprising that the polyanthus growers of the West Country have not cultivated them on a commercial scale for the cut-flower market. Other forms are Jack-a-napes, of hose-in-hose formation but having green stripes on each ruff, while the Jack-a-napes on Horseback is of similar form but with a tuft of coloured leaves directly beneath the bloom. This striped form possibly takes its name from a striped coat which was the fashion in the mid-seventeenth century. In his diary dated 5th July 1660, Samuel Pepys writes, 'This morning my brother Tom brought me my Jackanapes coat.'

Of Jack-a-napes on Horseback Gerard says in his Herbal '. . . whose flowers are curled and wrinkled after a most strange manner which our women have named Jack-a-napes on horseback.' In a book of the early Stuart days the author describes the same flower as 'all green and jagged'. The significant word seems to be 'wrinkled' or 'jagged'.

A Gally Gaskin is yet another distinct type of our native primrose, having an enlarged calyx and a frilled ruff beneath the bloom. The Gally Gaskin designation appears obvious if we inspect a certain picture of Henri Coiffier de Ruse, Marquis de Cinq-Mars, the frilled ruff beneath the knees aptly illustrating the flower of that name. Each of these delightful forms may be found growing in the wild state if one has the time and patience to look around the districts noted for their primroses.

We make no apology for these descriptions of the common primrose and its forms, for this is a book that aims at glorifying *Primula vulgaris*, just as Gerard and Parkinson and Rea did some four hundred years ago. Of recent years lengthy books by learned authorities have dealt with the Asiatic and European primrose and the Auricula, with scarcely a mention of our own native flower and its many delightful forms, far more pleasing to the eyes of an Englishman than any of the Asiatic importations, however colourful they may be. How delightful it is to know that posies of primroses have never ceased to be sold in the streets of London, century after century, bringing a welcome breath of rural England to the weary city dweller in springtime. But how much more fascinating it would be to see the equally old-world hose-in-hose or the lovely doubles sold in bunches too. Perhaps they soon will be, for the renewal of interest in the primrose seems to be bound up with a new phase in floral decoration. The little 'posie bowls' of the sixteenth century once again bring delight to our homes, and small flowering plants in bowls have taken the place of heavy foliage plants.

The polyanthus and its various forms, and in its brilliant modern art shades, becomes more popular year by year. What more lovely

Double Primroses, Madame Pompadour
and alba plena
from an old print

Primroses on the Rockery: var. Purple Splendour

subject for window boxes and for the small town garden, which must be planned in terms of small, compact and colourful plants, than these hardy plants of true rural-England flavour! The primrose is not only suitable for the small gardens of post-war years, it is also taking the place it merits as the ideal townsman's flower. It will multiply rapidly, established plants covering themselves with a mass of bloom at a time when the city dweller longs for a breath of the countryside, and it is prone to very few diseases; more important still, the habit these plants have of dying back over winter will preserve the foliage from soot deposits caused by the usual fog-laden atmosphere of the mid-winter months. Yet for all that, at this time of the year, they may still give us an occasional splash of colour. In a certain garden in north Staffordshire, those lovely *Juliae* varieties Dinah, Avalon and E. R. Janes are always a riot of colour all winter, and by the end of January, the first signs of the coming spring are apparent. The minute pale green leaves of the new season are showing above the soil and that earliest of all primroses, Mauve Queen, so lovely for posies, is soon to be a mass of colour after a long period of fog, frost, ice and snow.

The ability of the modern primrose and polyanthus to stand up to all conditions of soil and climate is contributing greatly to its popularity. In all corners of the world we come across the occasional plant, making a brave effort in spite of severe drought or intense cold. In a letter to the Royal Horticultural Society *Journal* of January 1952, Mr. D. G. Barton, writing from British Columbia, says; 'Kamloops, in British Columbia, is situated in what is known as the "Dry Belt", the rainfall averaging only 8 inches each year. The soil, for the most part very sandy, overlies strata of rock or boulders. I was amazed to find that polyanthus and *Primula acaulis* grow to perfection. Some of the best blooms came from gardens where plants grow in full sun with no shade at any time.' To quote Mr. Barton again: 'During the winter of 1949–50 the thermometer dropped to 40° below zero, with only a scant covering of snow. I saw many varieties of bloom the following spring and they were very fine indeed. Even the lengths of stems were excellent.' What other plants would be able to stand up to 70° of frost without any protection, and five months later to temperatures reaching 100° F., and bloom to perfection year after year?

Primula veris, the common cowslip, and its more robust relative the oxlip or *Primula Elatior*, may also be associated with the gardens of old. *Primula Elatior* is the more important of the two, in that it is the parent of our modern polyanthus, a subject so popular that nurserymen devote much of their time to its production for cut-flower sale or to the raising of the plants for garden decoration. The polyanthus, in its present form, is of more recent introduction, the old gold-laced form being the most sought-after during the nineteenth century. During post-war years the strains have improved out of all recognition, pale, indistinct colours now being replaced by the most brilliant tints.

It was the poet John Clare who told us of another of the primrose's most useful qualities, its willingness to be transplanted at any time of the year, even when in full bloom. Clare was the son of a labourer, who took up farming and failed. His delightful poem 'Cowslips and Primroses' was written a hundred years ago, and refreshing reading it is in this Atomic Age.

> *The cottager when coming home from plough*
> *Brings home a cowslip root in flower to set,*
> *Thus ere the Christmas goes, the spring is met . . .*

On many occasions must a ploughman, possibly John Clare himself, have carefully lifted from the hedgerow a root of some unusual primrose or cowslip, and, before removing his boots in the evening, have planted it in a corner of his cottage garden as dusk fell. Being herbs, the primrose and the cowslip were grown chiefly as ingredients for wine making, just as other herbs were cultivated for their medicinal properties, and also for their fragrance. Joined by the violet, the lily and the rose, herbs were always in great demand for scattering, in their dried form, about the damp, insanitary earthen floors of castles, manors and even churches.

During the days of the fortified house, the only plants cultivated were the herbs and these few flowers esteemed for their fragrance, and they were grown inside the fortified walls. Gardens, as we know them to-day, first came into being during the peaceful reign of Henry Tudor. Continual strife at home gave men little encouragement to make a garden, but with the death of Richard at Bosworth in 1485, a new era was about to dawn in England. Trade with the continent on a scale never before contemplated brought new wealth and happiness to the country, and it was not long before every manor and cottage had its own small garden. The first gardens took the form of knotted-beds, small beds planted with herbs, violets and primroses and joined or knotted together by miniature hedges of box, the narrow paths being made of coloured sand and gravel. The primrose and cowslip occupied an important place in the Tudor knot garden on account of their early flowering, for the gardens were made to yield their quota of flowers all the year round, and these flowers, together with the herbs, were used in cooking, for wine making, for health medicines and tonics, and for placing about the rooms of the badly-ventilated houses. Thomas Tullis, the sixteenth-century writer, includes both the cowslip and the primrose in his list of plants suitable for purifying the air.

As late as the beginning of the nineteenth century the primrose was still cultivated for its medicinal properties. In *The Family Herbal*, written by Sir John Hill, M.D., in 1812, we read '. . . the root is used. The juice of it snuffed up the nose occasions sneezing and is a good remedy against the headache. The dried root powdered has the same effect, but not so powerfully.'

Right through the sixteenth century members of the primrose family were grown in every garden; indeed Parkinson, in his *Paradisi*, mentions not only the hose-in-hose, double sulphur and double green, but also the auricula; of the 'purple cowslips or Beares eares' he had found at least twenty different varieties: tawny, blush and hair-coloured were represented in his collection.

Gardens kept their early Tudor form until about thirty years of the eighteenth century had passed, at which time the Dutch influence began to make itself felt, and Vanbrugh, Capability Brown and Batty Langley introduced the 'grand manner' to our gardens, a period of vast domains, of Wardour and Wentworth Woodhouse, of Croome Court and Kedleston. Langley's treatises on gardening, published in 1728, had as lengthy title, *New Prin-*

ciples of Gardening . . . after a more Grand Manner than has been done before, which meant that the dainty primrose was to be replaced by avenues of trees; the stream by the graceful fountain; the cottage window by the orangery, or conservatory as we know it to-day.

And yet, the poets of the eighteenth century still clung to the delicate bloom of the primrose; it was fast disappearing from our gardens but not from the banks and hedgerows. Oliver Goldsmith wrote these delightful lines just on two hundred years ago:

> *Her modest looks the cottage might adorn*
> *Sweet as the primrose peeps beneath the thorn.*

This lovely flower had returned to the environment it best enjoyed, the shade and shelter and the humus-laden soil of the cottage garden, which could now be found only under more natural conditions.

The introduction of the polyanthus just about sounded the death knell to the primrose family, for here was a florist's flower, and it quickly received the attention which in the past had been bestowed on the primrose. During the mid-nineteenth century, wide use of the gold-laced polyanthus was made in designs for pottery. Indeed, these charming flowers are incorporated with life-like precision on two fire panels of china which adorn the study of Major Taylor at his lovely home in Shropshire. These panels are one pair of a hundred made by the famous firm of Copeland and Garrett about the year 1850 and must be about the only pair of this design now in existence.

The reign of Victoria was also the reign of antimacassars and aspidistras, of the stiff geranium and the calceolaria, which matched the Victorian temperament. Once again the primrose was banished to the hedgerow where they, again to quote John Clare:

> *Behind the wood's old roots, where ivy shields*
> *Their crimpled, curdled leaves, will shine and hide.*

Hide their charm they certainly did, then at the end of the century interest revived for a number of reasons. First the Dean Brothers, Alexander and Richard, devoted considerable energy to hybridizing the wild primrose, then called *Primula acaulis*, but now known as *Primula vulgaris*. In 1882, *Primula acaulis*, Harbinger, a lovely white primrose, received an award and even to-day Dean's Hybrids is a most excellent strain of the common wild primrose, giving us this flower in a large range of delightful shades. A few years later, the Cocker Brothers were reintroducing the doubles at their famous Aberdeen nursery, the birth of the Bon Accords was taking place; but even more important the beautiful *Juliae* primroses reached this country from the Caucasus at the turn of the century. This wine-red primrose was to be the forerunner of a large range of brilliantly coloured and robust varieties, all containing *Juliae* blood. The lovely salmon-pink E. R. Janes, the claret-coloured Wanda, and the pale yellow Dorothy are ideal plants for town garden, window-box or rockery. From many of these *Juliae* hybrids we have a number of equally lovely 'sports', the sky-blue variety, Blue Horizon, being a superb dwarf primrose. Primroses were now coming back to favour, especially with the huge array of provincial gardeners who formed the backbone of the horticultural world. The small town garden had taken the place of the fifteenth-century cottage garden, and as it was able to combat deposits of soot and was almost completely free from disease, the *modern* single primroses now received much the same attention as did the old-fashioned doubles. The polyanthus still held its place in our affection, and where conditions allowed, was being widely used for naturalizing rather than for planting in regular beds, as also were the primroses introduced by the Dean Brothers. The garden of the twentieth century had completed the cycle. We must not forget, either, that the new century was opening up new horizons to travellers, and from parts of Asia a new range of Asiatic primroses was being introduced to Britain and western Europe.

But it is the true primrose that has most interest for us, with its single and double forms and its many lovely hybrids and species growing in our own British Isles. From Ireland come the charming bronze-leaved Garryarde primroses from the district bearing that name, and a host of other dainty types; indeed Ireland may be called the home of the primrose, which is common to these isles, in much the same way that Kashmir is the home of the now popular Asiatic primulas. We have to-day an array of new varieties and types, such as the hose-in-hose of true polyanthus form, which are proving just as popular as were the old hose-in-hose and doubles of Tudor gardens.

But what of these old varieties? Until very recently, they had almost ceased to exist, and it is only through the endeavour of one or two enthusiasts (William Chalmers, Mrs. McMurtrie, Mrs. Emmerson and Margery Fish come to mind) that these lovely old flowers have been rediscovered in out-of-the-way places and are being given their rightful place in our cottage and town gardens once more. The old red double Madame Pompadour, known two hundred years ago, was retraced in a Cheshire cottage garden, where it flourished in soil containing a large proportion of decayed beech and oak leaves; a fine crimson-laced Jack-in-the-Green of Tudor origin came from an Irish garden; and a crimson hose-in-hose, known to the sixteenth-century gardener, Gerard, by the name of 'double cowslip—having one flower within another', was found in an old Devonshire manor-house garden. This variety is to-day known as Sparkler, a wonderful primrose which will bloom in an exposed garden throughout the winter, completely unprotected. Perhaps Gerard knew this by the name of 'double cowslip, because it bears its bloom on a cowslip-like stem; and it is this characteristic that led various sixteenth-century writers to refer to the woodland primrose as 'the cowslip'.

Lack of interest, rather than lack of knowledge, appears to have been the most effective reason why the old-fashioned primroses almost passed out of cultivation. The old plants were just left to take care of themselves, and for want of periodical lifting and dividing they gradually died back. It is said by many to-day that most of these old favourites are difficult to cultivate. This, we are certain, has nothing to do with the plant losing stamina; rather would it appear to be due to lack of the correct amount of humus, sparsely provided in many gardens of to-day. The modern *Juliae* varieties can stand up to present-day soil conditions, because they have known no other, whereas the old favourites, especially the doubles, never seem to get accustomed to having to exist in a soil almost entirely devoid of humus and nitrogen content. Under the same conditions that existed in Tudor gardens these very same varieties could flourish to-day, and do so. In full sun, in a soil containing a very small proportion of humus, the *Juliae* hybrids should grow well, and the plants will quickly cover themselves with a mass of brilliantly coloured flowers. They will also grow well on the rockery. Those who are fortunate enough to be able to cultivate their primroses in a soil containing plenty of humus, and in the partial shade of an orchard, or in a north border, will find that the so-called 'difficult' primroses will flourish as they did in the reign of Elizabeth the First.

Nearly all primroses are useful for cutting and bunching, ideal subjects for the home. Now that the primrose has once again established itself in its rightful place, we may look with interest for the introduction of more wonderful varieties from our specialist growers. One colour that should reach perfection in the next year or so is the eagerly sought blue. It was in 1878 that G. F. Wilson of Wisley began to work on the production of a true blue primrose and this was accomplished twelve years later, but only during recent years has the colour become controlled to any degree, and the true blue polyanthus of fixed colour has still to become a reality.

What of the Auricula, a member of this same delightful primula family? Though it has never attained quite the same degree of popularity as the polyanthus and the primrose hybrids, it has never experienced the same ups and downs as the old double and hose-in-hose forms of the primrose. A native of the Alps, the plant first reached this country when the Flemish weavers settled here about the year 1575. Suffolk and south Lancashire were the favoured districts, and quickly the fame of the plant began to be known far and wide. This was of course the type known to-day as the Alpine Auricula. We have already seen that Parkinson knew the plant well in 1640, and John Rea in his *Flora*, published a quarter of a century later, provides the earliest detailed account of the plant; indeed, he mentions a number of enthusiasts who are already engaged on raising new varieties. Twenty years later, Sir Thomas Hanmer lists forty named auriculas in his *Garden Book*.

It was in south Lancashire, Cheshire and the north Staffordshire area that auricula cultivation took its strongest hold and it has remained so right up to the present day. The northern section of the National Auricula and Primula Society holds its annual show in Manchester during the first Saturday in May each year.

By the beginning of the nineteenth century, the show auriculas were becoming a familiar sight in our gardens and greenhouses, and on the show bench too, for an extraordinary change had come over the flower—a new type of auricula had come into existence with two quite new characteristics. The edges of the blooms were of a grey, green or white colour, while in the centre was a zone of white meal, or 'paste' of a most delicate texture; this led to this type of auricula being known as a 'show' type, and to prevent damage to the flowers the plants began to be grown in small pots under frames and in the greenhouse. By 1828 a series of coloured prints of Sweet's *Florist Guide* show that the plant had almost reached perfection.

None contributed more to the success of the auricula than the weavers of Lancashire and the miners of north Staffordshire, who with their auriculas and with their gooseberries of immense size, carried all before them at the local shows. Indeed, the auricula was the first plant ever to have its own society. A hundred years later, the auricula is still cultivated in this area, but the exhibition chrysanthemum and gladiolus have now tended to stake first claim on the interest of the gardeners of the North Midlands.

To-day, an array of enthusiasts and raisers of new primulas and auriculas are doing much to give these lovely spring flowers their rightful place in the gardens of England. For primroses we have William Chalmers of Aberdeen, Henry Jeffery of Yelverton, and that great enthusiast Captain Hawkes of Nantwich. With auriculas C. G. Haysom, R. H. Briggs, the Rev. Oscar Moreton, Dr. Hough and Tom Meek all toil long hours to bring this plant to perfection. The polyanthus, too, has its devoted followers, particularly the great plant houses of Blackmore and Langdon, and Suttons, and so we may look forward to more lovely varieties in the years ahead. This is to be the era of the small flowering plant and the primrose will resume its honoured place in our gardens once again.

CHAPTER II

The Cultivation of Single Primroses

One of the easiest of all plants to grow, the primrose (and here we include the *acaulis* and *Juliae* hybrids) and polyanthus should present no difficulties even to the novice gardener. The plants may be set out at any period of the year, and with a little care as to watering and perhaps some shading they will thrive. We know of no other plant that is so accommodating in this way; even when carrying a large amount of bloom and purchased from a store or market stall, where plants rarely receive the best of treatment, members of the primrose family may be expected to continue to bloom in all their glory in the weeks ahead. In the town garden, covered with a film of soot the whole year round, and with a soil that will mostly be a loam of poor quality, primroses will rarely be put off by their surroundings and adverse conditions. For window boxes, too, they are ideal subjects for spring colour, especially those varieties that flower on a polyanthus stem. In cold, exposed positions the plants which appear to be so delicate but which really are so strong. will invariably put up a brave show and will give at least an odd flower to help to brighten the dreary January days, even when the icy north winds burn the foliage and leave the ground as hard as iron. How often have we seen the long neat row of Primula Wanda as an edging to a path in many a town garden, a brilliant mass of claret and green during the most dreary period of springtime, the cushion-like foliage of the plants completely hidden by the abundance of the bloom. What other plant would put up so exciting a profusion under like conditions? For the town garden, the hardy primroses have no equal for a spring display and are rarely troubled by changes of temperature or conditions in which almost any other plant would succumb or produce a most bedraggled show of blossom.

In the cottage garden, containing almost always a fair amount of humus, and shaded by the fruit trees and shrubs which are found in most country gardens, the primroses will give a magnificent display. In the authors' gardens, partially shaded by old apple trees, the two hundred or more varieties of primroses, planted in massed formation, produce a wealth of colour from March until early June, quite without rival for miles around. Here the soil is of a light loam and contains little fresh manure, but a certain amount of humus is continually formed by the ever-falling leaves of the apple trees, and augmented by a small amount of peat and old mushroom-bed manure. Here, then, the plants are growing under conditions they obviously enjoy, a humid atmosphere and warm spring sunshine that quickly transform the stark branches of the apple trees into a fairyland of pink and white blossom. Partial shade primroses enjoy, but not full shade; they must have sunshine and some moisture, which they cannot obtain if planted directly under large trees during summer time. Indeed they will produce their most brilliant colours only when the sun shines on them for a long period of the day. Partial shade will encourage length of stem but sunshine will enhance the rich velvety colours of the blooms. The double-flowering varieties appreciate a greater degree of shade, for their colours are more delicate and the plants are never as tolerant to draught as are the singles of the *Juliae* varieties, But this shade should be provided in the form of a mulch, using peat or leaf mould during a prolonged spell of sunshine, or as soon as the plants have finished flowering in May. At all times, watering must be attended to. North of Birmingham, unless summer conditions are particularly severe, little or no watering will be necessary, though the plants will welcome a mulch. This will take the place of the grassy banks on which the primrose roots are always happiest, their roots sheltered, and the flower open to the sunlight. How often do we see a railway bank a vivid mass of primrose in springtime? Surely the explanation for the plant's flourishing under such conditions is the stony nature of the ground, the stones acting like a mulch and providing the roots with cool, damp conditions. Certainly such a position offers little humus, but the stones are acting in much the same way. In such sites and in the hedgerow the plant blooms to perfection year in, year out, the action of worms on the falling hedgerow leaves furnishing the desired humus content. In such conditions the plant will require almost no attention other than a division of the roots every two to three years. In those gardens where cultural conditions reproducing the natural haunt of the primrose cannot be provided, it will repay the grower to work into the soil a quantity of humus-forming material. The single primroses and polyanthus, while appreciating as much humus as it is possible to provide for them, will flower to perfection over a number of years with the minimum amount, a far less quantity than will be necessary for the double-flowered varieties. A small quantity of well-rotted manure mixed with a small amount of granulated peat and well worked into the soil will provide the humus required to produce a brilliant display. Decayed oak and beech leaves, and of course leaf mould, are all suitable subjects as well as composted garden rubbish, provided it is not in a sticky condition. Lawn mowings which tend to become sticky should always first be mixed with leaf mould or peat. No other fertilizer will be required, though where a soil has a high humus content, an artificial with a nitrogen content may be found valuable. Polyanthus plants grown for cut-flower purposes should have a slightly larger amount of rotted manure added, for they will be expected to produce a large quantity of bloom on a sturdy, well-formed stem, and may even be required to stand gentle forcing under cloches or frames.

It is said that to maintain their vigour and flower to perfection over the years, all forms of the primrose family must be given liberal quantities of nitrogen, and that they are gross feeders. While this may be true of the doubles (and to produce these well the American growers use large quantities of cotton seed meal in their soils to supply the necessary nitrogen) the single varieties and hose-in-hose do not seem to require anything more, provided that the humus content of the soil is adequate. The polyanthus seem to fall somewhere between the singles and doubles: they are reasonably large feeders but not nearly so large as many of the doubles. One grower of the doubles on a commercial scale now uses wool shoddy as a means of providing both humus and nitrogen for the plants.

The soil for window boxes or troughs in which the hardy primroses appear so much at ease should consist of a light loam with which a small quantity of peat or leaf mould has been incorporated. The whole should be thoroughly mixed before being placed into the boxes in a friable condition. The soil should be changed every year before the plants are in the early bud state, which will be the most suitable time for transplanting from the border or bed. During very sunny weather, window boxes facing any direction except the north will require regular attention as to watering, for the soil must never be allowed to dry out completely.

After the soil has been enriched and deeply dug it should be brought to a fine tilth before any planting is done. Even the smallest piece of rootstock will grow, and where expensively rare old-fashioned varieties are being grown and increased it may be necessary to utilize even the smallest piece of root; and these will not flourish in a soil which does not come into close contact with every portion of the root. Detailed methods of propagation are given in the following chapter.

Primroses and polyanthus may be planted out at any time. Plants have been set out during a bleak January day, when an area of snow had first to be moved away from above the soil. Early spring is a suitable time, for the showery weather generally enjoyed is always appreciated by the young plants. In the south and west country, February planting may be considered most satisfactory. The young plants will quickly become established and come into bloom in a few weeks' time. In the north, late August is believed to be the best planting time. June, immediately after flowering, is generally a dry, sunny month and is not a suitable time for primroses to be moved, but by mid-August the weather tends to become wet the plants have had a rest following ten weeks of flowering, and then is the most suitable planting time to allow the plants to become firmly established before the severe weather of winter sets in. But the commercial grower and the amateur with a large collection may have to carry out division and planting almost the whole year round, and here no plant could be more co-operative or easier to increase.

Early autumn is the best period to plant the polyanthus so that it will become thoroughly established before winter and come into profitable cutting or give a brilliant display early in spring. Both the primrose and polyanthus should be set out only when the weather is showery, though the soil should never be waterlogged or sticky. A soil which could be described as of a clay nature should be given an amount of sand or grit in addition to the humus, for no member of the primrose family likes a waterlogged soil; possible exceptions are several of the Asiatic group, and even by these plants a cold sticky soil is not tolerated.

Set out the plants about nine inches apart, spreading out the root and drawing the soil right up to the crown of the plant. The soil should be made quite firm by treading or pressing by hand. Should the weather be sunny, with a drying wind, bracken, straw or branches should be placed over the plants until they appear firmly established. During the months of September to March there will be no need to give protection unless it be to the more 'difficult' varieties during extremely severe weather. It is said that as a race, the primula family will not tolerate lime, that the plants will not grow successfully over a chalky soil. This may be true of certain species, especially many of the Asiatic primulas, but as far as the ordinary European primrose is concerned, we have always found that they are little troubled by lime in the soil; though they do seem to enjoy best a soil that is slightly acid in nature. In this respect, and with their love of a little shade at the roots, the primrose is very much like the strawberry plant.

Those growing for exhibition should lift the established plants as soon as the first signs of fresh growth are apparent. Chiefly depending upon the weather, these are generally observed early in February, the tiny bright green of the leaves just showing above the soil.

The 60 size pot is the most suitable and into this is placed a compost made up of well-rotted turf loam to which has been added a small quantity of well-decomposed manure and some horticultural peat. In this the plants are potted and placed in a cold frame, or back into the ground in the hole from where the plant was removed. When growing for exhibition, it is necessary to produce a plant which will not only bear a mass of bloom well worthy of putting on display, but one which will also have its bloom in perfect condition on exhibition day, and that calls for considerable care and experience in retarding the selected plants, this being done by shading the plants with sacking whenever a strong sun shines.

Primroses will grow anywhere, but because of their great powers of accommodation, it should not be taken that the plants will do themselves full justice in poor surroundings. One frequently sees the plant putting up a brave struggle in the worn-out soil of a town-garden shrubbery, under some laurel bushes maybe, where it will never attain the desired beauty it is possible for it to put forth; and the most 'choosey' doubles will not survive at all. And of course the plant provides a more pleasant picture when it can be planted in its natural setting, say in clumps on a grassy bank, in a spinney of silver birch, or in a partially shaded part of a garden where it may be allowed to produce its delicately perfumed bloom undisturbed. In the garden of one of the writers is a small but steep grass bank, where young apple trees are planted, and it is here that primroses bloom in all their glory. There are almost a hundred varieties planted here in small clumps of two or three roots, and there they are left undisturbed year after year. Crocus and miniature daffodils grow amongst them and during April and May the bank is a riot of colour, the bloom appearing just above the grass; as the bloom tends to die away the grass becomes longer, thus affording protection to the roots from the stronger summer sun, and an additional shield during the winter. It is, however, advisable either to run a motor or hand scythe over the grass during July to prevent growth from becoming too rank and thereby choking the primroses.

Those who possess a herbaceous border may have an attractive edging by using that delightful primrose, Lady Greer, with its heads of tiny lemon yellow flowers, fairy-like in the spring sunshine, or the Irish hose-in-hose, Lady Lettice, which is a strong grower and bears pale yellow blooms, flushed with apricot. This variety has the advantage of remaining in bloom almost the whole year round. Lady Greer is at its loveliest early in the evening of a still April day, when a row of thousands of tiny flowers will appear most attractive; and they also possess the delicate true primrose perfume. Such varieties make a most pleasing change from the everlasting Wanda, however lovely it may be. Another splendid border variety, and so excellent for a window box too, is Fair Maid, in our opinion one of the loveliest primroses in existence. The heads of bloom are borne on stems nine to ten inches in length, stems of a rich magohany red, and the blooms are of vivid orange-rust and have a unique double yellow centre. It hails from Scotland, and why it is not in every garden we do not know, for it is at its best early in May when there are few flowers about.

For a late spring display there is no plant to equal the modern strains of polyanthus which have advanced out of all recognition since Miss Gertrude Jekyll first seriously took them up. Those who have seen growing the terra-cottas and bright reds of the Brilliancy strain, in drifts among young silver birch trees, will never forget the experience. For more formal garden display, the bedding strains make a superb show and are exceedingly long lasting.

The use of primroses for spring bedding provides a most original and pleasing effect. Try planting the colourful Primula Romeo with its large pansy-like blooms of pure parma-violet, under a bed set out with that lovely pale-yellow Cottage Tulip, Mother's Day; or plant the royal purple Frühlingzauber under a pure white tulip.

The great value of these two single primroses is that as well as providing a carpet of lavish colour in the more exposed districts and in town gardens, they will rapidly increase themselves from the small off-set stage to a cabbage-size plant within two years. Should the same bed be required for a summer bedding display, then the primroses may be lifted with the bulbs and planted in a piece of spare ground where they are divided and left untouched until required again the following late autumn.

One of the most outstanding displays of the spring garden may be obtained by carpeting a bed of white daffodils with one of the very dwarf-growing crimson primroses, e.g. Crimson Queen, Sunset Glow, or the flame-coloured Afterglow. The effect is truly one of great beauty. In the north and in the more exposed positions of Britain the primrose is far more reliable than the wallflower, which forms only spindly, weak-flowering plants in most exposed gardens. The contrast between the dwarf, vividly coloured primroses and the taller bulbs is most attractive. Daffodil lovers would be well advised to try a carpeting of the magnificent sky blue primrose, Blue Horizon, beneath a bed of King Alfred daffodils; both bloom at the same time and the effect is almost staggering. The cream-coloured varieties are also most showy when planted amongst Muscari bulbs; the contrast of the cream hose-in-hose, Lady Lettice or Erin's Gem, growing amongst Muscari, Cambridge Blue is a delightful adornment for the rockery or even for the window box.

Owing to their ability to withstand moving when in bud or bloom, primroses are ideal window box plants. Their powers of resistance against winter conditions and soot deposits of a town also enable them to be planted in the boxes at any time between October and March. They will give an unusual and charming effect if planted with the lovely miniature daffodils and muscari; or a very early variety such as the beautiful wine-red Joan Schofield will come into bloom with the Snowdrops, the red and white in striking contrast. But whatever the display that is being arranged, care must be taken to ensure that the various plants or bulbs come into bloom at the same time, and for this reason the time of flowering has been given with the single varieties. The doubles are not so suitable for bedding purposes, chiefly because they are more expensive to buy and take a longer time to make good-sized plants, while they are also more exacting in their cultural requirements. There are several exceptions, the century-old Marie Crousse making a large plant and flowering profusely under all reasonable conditions; and the old white, *alba plena*, is similar. Quaker's Bonnet, a pure mauve, is also very easy and quickly makes a large plant. But few of the doubles possess the vivid colouring of some of the new singles such as Tawny Port, Afterglow, Betty Green and Fair Maid.

Juliae Primrose, Charles Bloom

Garryarde Primrose, var. Guinevere

The Cultivation of Single Primroses

One of the most enchanting spring flowering displays to be seen of recent years was noticed in a Sussex garden where single primroses were planted in wheel-shaped rows. In this particular instance the plants were all in bloom together, the colours being placed so that as great a contrast as possible was obtained. A more satisfactory display would possibly be achieved with plants coming into bloom at intervals, commencing with Mauve Queen in early March and ending with Felicity early in May.

A square or oblong bed would be equally effective, and one idea would be to keep the colour scheme to various shades of mauves and purples. Those who favour the Elizabethan knot-garden may produce a most pleasing effect by using dwarf box hedging in a simple design and filling the inner space with quaint primroses of various forms. The doubles, hose-in-hose and Jack-in-the-Greens may be used.

Those who use window boxes, tubs and troughs will find that the taller-growing varieties will provide the most colourful display, for they will hold their bloom above the level of the box. For this reason, Fair Maid, Lady Greer and the new polyanthus hose-in-hose are most suitable choices.

The possibilities which these delightful primroses offer are inexhaustible. They should be more widely used, especially by our Corporations for spring bedding schemes, where hardiness and the minimizing of labour are primary considerations. Perhaps the only reason why these plants are not more generally grown is the attention the early spring buds receive from the sparrows of our towns. From the gardens of Buckingham Palace to those of the smallest 'pre-fab', sparrows do make themselves nuisances where primroses grow, and especially when those first spring buds are showing colour, and it is the odd plants that they seem to pick out and devastate. Those who keep a cat will have no trouble from sparrows, but what of the others? Strong thread stretched over the plants will definitely keep the pests away, but thread is not lasting, and as a better alternative, Mr. Hills has suggested the use of very fine wire used for winding transformers. Yet another alternative is the use of 'Glitterbangs' marketed by Chase Protected Cultivation Ltd. I have tried two or three of these in a town garden

C

with good effect. The countryman will encounter no trouble from sparrows, simply on account of the much wider range of new buds to be found in the hedgerows and gardens during spring; and where plants are set out *en masse* there appears to be only a very limited amount of damage. Much the same trouble besets the crocus every spring; like the primrose it is evidently as eagerly awaited by the sparrows as by the gardener!

CHAPTER III

Propagation of Primroses

Polyanthus and primrose plants are readily increased by division of the roots and by seed sowing. Many of the rare double varieties may also be increased from pieces of rootstock, rather like the herbaceous iris, but it is by division that the named varieties are increased. Those required for cut-flower production and for bedding in large numbers may be readily grown from seed. The hybridizer, too, relies on the sowing of seed to introduce his new varieties. Many of the Asiatic primulas readily increase themselves by sowing their own seed, but Shakespeare's 'Pale primroses' of the English hedgerows rarely set their own seed and rely chiefly on the increasing of the root stock.

We know of no easier plant for propagation than the single-flowered primrose. In twelve months a tiny root will have become a huge clump, tuft or cushion, whichever description of an established primrose root is preferred. This may be divided into as many as twenty small offsets which, if planted under moist conditions, will quickly re-establish themselves. Some varieties will increase more rapidly than others, while some are easier to divide into small offsets. Primroses of the Wanda type increase rapidly and when dug up, with the soil shaken from the roots, the plant will readily divide by slight pressure of the fingers at the base of the leaves. A number of varieties are more easily divided with the aid of a sharp knife which is used to cut up the root into sections, each containing a crown (rather like dividing a rhubarb root). The moment for carrying out this division will depend much on the weather, for moist conditions will ensure a more quickly established plant. It is said that the best time is immediately after the plants have finished flowering, some time in early June that is, a time when they would shed their seed under natural conditions. This may be so under the moist conditions of the hedgerow or along the banks of a stream, but June is frequently a month of drought in the town garden, and the soil will have been drained of much of its moisture by the mid-summer sun. A far better time for the work appears to be late in August in the north country, for then the young plants will become established before winter commences in earnest. In the south and west country, planting and division of the roots should take place late in autumn, for here the weather is never unduly severe, and in his exposed garden on the north-east coast one of the authors plants out rooted divisions from August until the end of March. But it should be remembered that the primrose will divide and flourish even when in full bloom, and also during January when the foliage would seem to have disappeared altogether. Divisions will readily have become established in any soil that is retentive of moisture, and here a little peat or leaf mould will help enormously while the young plants establish themselves, and so, too, will planting into partially shaded land. How often to divide is a matter which frequently gives cause for concern. As a rule of thumb it should be said that polyanthus and garden primroses of the single and hose-in-hose types will need lifting and dividing every two or three years. If allowed to remain undivided for a longer period, the centre portions of the plant will probably begin to die back, and these will ultimately be lost in cultivation. When growing commercially the plants will generally be lifted in the late summer of each year and be divided into plants that will be of good saleable size by the following spring. Almost all amateur enthusiasts prefer to purchase and plant their primroses when in bloom or in the bud state. A much better time would be in autumn so that the plants become established and do not lose much of their vitality when they are moved in full bloom.

While a three-yearly division of the single primrose and polyanthus is most suitable for these plants, double primroses should be divided more frequently; for if allowed to remain undivided for a long period, they will quickly die back. They also possess the habit of forming a thick, coarse rootstock which is apt to lift itself out of the ground. Should it suffer from lack of moisture as a result of this, it will quickly die off, for the new roots are formed above the old rootstock; and these will shrivel up in a dry period if the plants do not receive a mulch or if they are not replanted frequently. It is because of this that the reputation of the double primrose has suffered in recent years, and lack of division at the correct time has contributed greatly to the modern axiom that the doubles are 'difficult'.

Growing from seed is the hybridist's method of raising new varieties, and, is the ideal procedure for those who wish to raise a stock of primroses or polyanthus without undue expense. Where seed can be saved or obtained from an authentic source, the grower may occasionally be rewarded by a variety of outstanding merit. The primrose flower is particularly adapted to purposes of cross-pollination in that two types of flowers are produced. One throws up a pin-eyed stigma to the top of the petal tube, with the stamens half-way down the tube; in the other type the stamens are only just below the top of the tube, with the stigma half-way down. This being so, both bees and those insects having a long tongue readily pollinate each type of flower. Though pollination appears to be so thorough, the fact that few bees and other insects are about when the primrose is in full bloom means that cross-pollination of the earliest flowering varieties seldom occurs, and the flowers fail to set their seeds readily. Shakespeare alluded to this in his *A Winter's Tale* (as quoted on an earlier page):

> . . . *pale primroses*
> *That die unmarried, ere they can behold*
> *Bright Phoebus in his strength, a malady*
> *Most incident to maids.*

And Milton's *Lycidas* has a reference to

> . . . *the rathe primrose that forsaken dies.*

We put the matter more prosaically by pointing out once again that the primrose of our hedgerows increases by accumulation of the rootstock rather than by seed.

Where cross-pollination is carried out by hand, the aid of a camel hair brush is necessary, the work being done on a fine dry day. The single *Juliae* primroses, the hose-in-hose and the poly-anthus all produce pollen in abundance in their diverse varieties, but of the doubles, only Arthur Du Moulin and Prince Silver-wings appear to produce pollen in quantity. The pollen of these two varieties is therefore transferred to the chosen singles that are in bloom at the same time, and the plants should be in their first flush of bloom for best results. There are a number of varieties in bloom with the two mentioned doubles, but the earliest-flowering varieties such as Mauve Queen and *Altiaca grandiflora* will have already finished flowering. These early singles and hose-in-hose may be cross-pollinated by each other and of course so may the later-flowering varieties—of which Felicity, huge mauve, and Maureen Genders, mahogany red edged with white, are out standing. The pollen of the double varieties is transferred to the stigma of the singles; also with the singles themselves cross-pollination with each other is simplicity itself, if care is taken to mark the selected plants. In order to build up a robust strain, it is necessary to select only the very strongest, disease-free plants and plants that bloom to type. Small, weak-growing plants that may produce a bloom paler than the normal must not be used. No sign of disease should be present; in this respect, however, members of the primrose family suffer little.

In about a month the seed will have ripened and the round capsule that contains it will begin to burst, opening from the top into five compartments. It will be advisable to cover the selected plants with muslin as soon as pollination is complete, to prevent any further pollination by insects. Also it will be advisable to pollinate several flowers on each plant. As soon as the seed capsules appear to be bursting they should be carefully removed and placed on a sheet of plain white paper in a sunny room where they will thoroughly ripen and may then be emptied from the capsules. All pods and chaff must be discarded, for if sown with the seed they may cause trouble from moulds.

The process of pollinating is carried out in much the same way by all gardeners, but the sowing of the seeds is a more varied technique, there being two main schools of thought. One section suggests sowing the seed immediately after it has ripened, and that great authority on the primula, Mr. Kenneth Corsar, is one who suggests immediate sowing; yet others advise winter sowing and subjecting the seeds to a temperature below freezing point for a few days before germinating the seed in gentle heat during very early spring. Both methods follow nature and appear to be equally successful. The primrose native to the British Isles sheds its ripened seed during early summer, as indeed do those late-flowering varieties growing under natural conditions. The seed of the European *Juliae* types and many of the Asiatic primulas is first subject to conditions of snow and ice in the Alps, the Caucasus, and the Himalayas before warmer weather encourages germination.

Mrs. Florence Levy, of the famous Barnhaven Gardens in Oregon, U.S.A., suggests the use of a refrigerator for quick germination of the hard-coated primrose seed. Her method is to place a drop of water on the seed to moisten it, then place it in a transparent envelope, wrap in waxed paper, and place in a refrigerator for several days, taking out the seed at intervals, thawing it, then re-moistening and returning to the ice box. Experience has dictated that this procedure should take place in early April, using the seed saved from the previous summer. The seed is allowed to remain in the refrigerator for two to three days and is then sown into pans of prepared compost. The most suitable medium for even germination seems to be one composed of decayed turf loam to which is added approximately 20 per cent coarse sand and the same quantity of horticultural peat, which should be thoroughly moistened before being mixed in. Leaf mould may be used instead of the peat or half the quantity of peat and an equal amount of leaf mould. The John Innes Sowing Compost obtainable from most seed stores is equally suitable. First the pan or box must have a layer of broken stones or boiler ashes at the bottom to help drainage. Polyanthus seed, being more easily germinated, may be sown directly into cold frames or into the open ground in early April, preferably under cloches.

When the seed is removed from the refrigerator, it should be exposed for about half an hour to allow it to dry before sowing takes place. Then sow at once, scattering the seed on top of the compost which has been made level and firm. The seed should not be covered with soil, but should be given a gentle watering with hot (not boiling) water. This will hasten germination. The pans or boxes should be covered with a sheet of clean glass and be placed in the warm temperature of home or greenhouse until germination takes place. Where some form of heat can be employed the freezing and sowing may take place during March or even earlier, the contention being that it is more satisfactory to use seed in as fresh a condition as possible. Certainly old seed which has become hard will germinate only haphazardly, however carefully handled. Where only a frame is used for containing the seed pans, then it will be better to delay operations until early April or even later.

The pans should be shaded during sunny weather only, for though a strong sun will hasten germination, it may also cause the compost to become too dry, necessitating over-frequent applications of water which may tend to cause a damping off condition. Wherever possible the soil, like the casing soil of a mushroom bed, should remain in a slightly moist condition until the seeds have germinated and have produced plants large enough to handle. At no time should the compost be allowed to dry out completely, otherwise the germinating seed may be killed through lack of moisture. Daily, and in warm weather twice daily, the glass should be removed for moisture inspection. Shading must be given whenever it is thought to be necessary. After the first application of hot water, which must only be given before germination takes place, possibly the most satisfactory method of watering is to immerse the pans in tepid water for half an hour whenever necessary. This will prevent disturbance to the tiny seeds. Depending chiefly upon the temperature at which the seeds are germinated, there should be some form of plant life to be seen after about twenty days. If the weather is cold it may be a month or more before germination actually takes place. The seedlings, once visible above the soil, must be watered even more carefully than before germination takes place. Too much moisture makes for a damp, sticky condition of the soil and will only cause a number of the seedlings to damp off. Water only when the seedlings require it, and that requirement is governed by temperature conditions. Also remove the glass covering, otherwise the seedlings will be 'drawn'. Frequently seeds of primroses germinate unevenly. The greater the care taken over their sowing, the more reliable will be germination, but it is a good idea to allow the seedlings to remain in the pans undisturbed for as long as possible so as not to harm any seedlings that might only just be appearing. When the first seedlings have become large enough to handle, and when you have allowed them to remain undisturbed for as long as is feasible, lift them very carefully from the pans, disturbing the compost as little as possible. For when the first batch of seedlings have been moved the pans should again be covered with the sheet of glass, watered, and allowed to receive once more the same treatment that they were given when first the seed was sown. At intervals, and these may be long drawn out, other seedlings will appear, which may even develop into the very strongest and most attractive plants. It will be advisable to retain the pans for at least six months. Again, never discard the weak-looking plant, for this may develop into the best of them all.

The young plants should be potted singly into 2½-inch pots or into the 48 size, placing four in each; or they may be set out in deep seed boxes. If the small individual pots can be obtained, they will undoubtedly give a better plant and this is especially necessary when growing for exhibition.

The compost for potting should consist of turf loam to which have been added horticultural peat and sand and a small amount of very well rotted farmyard manure, provided it is not in a sticky condition. Old mushroom-bed compost, where it can be obtained, is ideal for primroses and may be liberally mixed in with loam to which is added a small quantity of sand.

After potting, the plants should be allowed to stand in an open frame, unless the weather is very cold, and in four weeks' time will be ready for the open ground or a larger pot. Constant attention must be given to watering, for should the weather be hot, shading of the plants will be necessary, as well as the creation of a humid atmosphere by spraying the plants twice a day, and by maintaining the supply of water. Planting out should only be done when the ground is in a moist condition, late April being a most suitable time, or failing this, late August.

From a batch of, say, fifty seedlings the hybridist will be fortunate if he obtains two plants that will produce a bloom that comes within the category of a first-class plant in either a double, single or hose-in-hose. But growers who increase the number in their collection of primroses by sowing seed will generally obtain a large proportion of plants that will provide interest and colour in the garden for many years to come.

Those who are raising the double varieties should note that the plants appear to produce the most reliable results from second-generation crosses, the first cross almost always throwing singles.

There are a number of primulas that will quite easily reproduce themselves by naturally sowing their own seed. The lovely *Primula rosea*, so useful in that it will thrive in dark, damp places, is one that if left undisturbed will sow its own seed which will germinate without much difficulty. Many of the Asiatics will do so, but here we are interested only in the native primrose.

To those who are raising the *Juliae* singles, it is suggested that the range of mauve, magenta and crimson shades appears to be sufficient, and unless something very outstanding in these colours is raised, those put forward for naming should be in the true-blue, yellow, white or some distinctive colours, for which the demand will be great.

CHAPTER IV

Some Lovely Single Primroses and Polyanthus

(1) First in bloom about March 7th.
(2) ,, ,, ,, ,, March 21st.
,, ,, ,, ,, April 1st.
(4) ,, ,, ,, ,, April 21st.
All ten to twelve days later in the North.

AFTERGLOW (3). Originating close to Drake's old home at Buckland in Devon, this is a superb new primrose, of rich rust-orange colour with a distinct eye. Having a long flowering season, it is possibly the finest variety ever introduced by Mr. Jeffery of the Champernowne Nurseries.

ALTIACA GRANDIFLORA (1). An old variety (from the Caucasus) but none the less attractive. Early to bloom, the flowers are of a pure mauve-pink of real primrose habit, and most prolific. Heralds the spring.

ANITA (2). A startling new primrose with its navy-blue blooms, suffused crimson, held above the foliage, almost like a cineraria. It is ideal for window boxes. Very long flowering. Lovely under trees.

AVALON (1). Enjoys shade, and when first seen by one of the writers was thought to be a bed of Princess of Wales violets, with which it is almost identical in its violet-blue colouring. A lovely new primrose, remaining in bloom for a very long period and very prolific indeed. Makes a lovely house plant in glass bowls in early April.

BARROWBY GEM (1). A handsome yellow polyanthus, much admired by H. M. The Queen Mother. Sweetly perfumed and one of the very first to bloom. Now very scarce.

43

BARTIMEUS (3). A very old variety, of polyanthus habit. The colour is dark red, with no eye. The old 'eyeless' primrose.

BEAMISH FOAM (2). A delightful primrose of polyanthus habit. The delicate pink blooms are splashed with pale yellow.

BETTY GREEN (1). A new Dutch variety having vivid claret-red blooms of medium size, very freely produced, and attractive rich apple-green foliage.

BLUE HORIZON (3). Found in a Kentish garden and introduced by Six Hills Nursery Ltd., Stevenage, and what a gem it is! The blooms are clear sky-blue, freely produced, and in habit like Wanda from which it is a 'sport'; it flowers for ever.

BLUE PRIMROSE (1). (Dark). A true Oxford blue.

BLUE PRIMROSE (1). (Pale.) A true Cambridge blue.

BRIDGET (4). Rich mauve-pink with large yellow eye. Very late and of very dwarf habit. An uncommon primrose and one of the last to bloom.

BUCKLAND BELLE (3). A Champernowne introduction, and a superb primrose of deep violet-blue flushed crimson and of extremely strong constitution.

BUNTY (2). Lovely deep-blue with large flowers freely produced over a long period. Has deep yellow eye.

CHARLES BLOOM (3). A superb variety, of polyanthus habit and very sturdy constitution. The blooms are of a rich velvet crimson-purple with deep orange eye and are freely produced. One of the best of the single primroses.

CHERRY (2). A new primrose, like E. R. Janes in habit, but with the bloom of an intense cherry-red colour. A much-needed colour.

CRADDOCK WHITE (2). A beautiful primrose and though the blooms are not so pure a white as Harbinger, it is of stronger constitution and holds its bloom more erect. Has attractive bronze foliage.

CRIMSON BEDDER (3). Very similar to Crimson Queen in colour, but is in bloom later and is more compact, though the bloom is not quite so large.

CRIMSON CUSHION (3). A delightful primrose for the rockery, being similar in habit to Purple Cushion, but with its flowers a rich red; of almost trailing habit.

CRIMSON GLORY (2). A wonderful new variety, it is of polyanthus formation with the huge individual blooms of a rich
crimson-red.

CRIMSON QUEEN (3). The largest of the crimson-red class
which possess a tinge of magenta colour. A lovely primrose with
pale apple-green foliage.

CRISPII (2). A lovely primrose, covering itself with a mass of
delicate mauve-pink bloom.

DAVID GREEN (1). Should be in every collection. The dark
burgundy-red blooms are very free and against the vivid emerald-
green foliage, with the evening sun behind, make a plant that is
outstandingly beautiful. A bloom with almost complete lack of
eye.

DINAH (2). A gem from Holland, remaining eight weeks in
bloom. The dainty blooms are like real velvet, burgundy-crimson
in colour, and have a unique olive-green eye. In bloom again in
late autumn when it is more colourful than any primrose.

DOROTHY (2). A rare pale lemon-yellow of excellent habit and
a long flowering season. Very strong grower. Has delightful
frilled petals, and flowers again in autumn. A really lovely primrose.

ELMHURST (2). A lovely polyanthus not too easily increased.
The bloom, held well above the foliage, is very early and of a
brilliant crimson-scarlet, with a deep buttercup-yellow eye.

EMPEROR (3). Another new variety having shining wine-purple
blooms with a large white centre and a white spot on the edge of
each petal.

E. R. JANES (2). An older variety, but what a beauty! A perfect rock primrose, for when in bloom it shows almost no foliage
—just a mass of salmon-pink blooms, flushed orange, slightly
scented and held in clusters to the sun. It flowers again in late
autumn and may remain in bloom over winter in a sheltered
garden.

FELICITY (4). Of polyanthus habit and though a shy little plant
is one of our favourites. The large frilled blooms are of a bright
rich purple-pink and have a distinct pale green eye. With Bridget,
one of the last to flower.

FAIR MAID (4). From the Perth district of Scotland, very late, but outstanding in every way. Of miniature polyanthus habit the blooms are of a rich vermilion-rust with a unique double yellow eye. The sturdy bronze stems make it a grand cut flower and most suitable for window box cultivation.

FLENE (1). Similar in colour and texture to Miss Massey, but the velvet-crimson blooms are of a unique shape.

FRÜHLINGZAUBER (1). Deep royal purple, the large flat blooms are held well above the foliage. The best true purple. A magnificent primrose of strong constitution and very free flowering. Increases rapidly.

FUCHSIA (3). Of a colour similar to a rich fuchsia-pink; of sturdy habit and with deep green leaves.

GARRYARDE, ENID (4). Similar in habit and freedom of flowering to its sister (see below), but with blooms of a much deeper pink, though not necessarily more beautiful.

GARRYARDE, GUINEVERE (4). A magnificent primrose having deep bronze foliage and large pink blooms held in clusters above the foliage. From the Garryarde district of Ireland.

GARRYARDE, THE GRAIL (3). A rare variety of attractive Elizabethan brick-red colour, with large yellow eye.

GARRYARDE, VICTORY (4). Another of this much-sought-after race from Ireland, with cucumber green leaves and attractive peony-purple blooms.

GLORIA (2). Glowing crimson-red on long sturdy stems. The petals have a distinct white vein on the insides. Very showy indeed, literally covering itself with a mass of glowing crimson.

GROENKEN'S GLORY (3). A Dutch variety of compact habit. The blooms are a bright mauve-pink with a unique green eye. One of the most attractive of all.

HARBINGER (1). Very early and now rare, bearing a large bloom of whitest white, but has not so strong a constitution as Craddock White. Famed for its earliness.

HILLHOUSE PINK (3). Has the unusual deep bronze foliage of the Garryarde primroses; and a pretty pale pink bloom. A very rare primrose.

HILLHOUSE RED (3). Similar to above, but has a bloom of rich crimson-port. Very sturdy growers are the Hillhouse varieties.

ICOMBE HYBRID (2). A rare primrose having bloom of a delightful rosy-mauve, colour freely produced.

IDEAL (4). A rather lovely variety, the deep crimson blooms, flushed orange, have a large orange-yellow eye which blends into the crimson. Tall growing and a fine border variety.

IRIS MAINWARING (2). Delicate pure pale blue, flushed pink. The foliage is deep green and the whole is of very compact habit. One of the best primroses and an ideal rockery plant.

JEWELL (3). A very free flowering crimson-purple, ideal for the rockery. A little gem amongst primroses.

JILL (2). An unusual little primrose rather like Tawny Port (see page 50) as to daintiness of habit; and the mauve blooms are quite flat in form.

JOAN SCHOFIELD (1). A superb new variety, one of the best half-dozen primroses in cultivation. Its huge blooms are wine-red, flushed vermilion, and have a large yellow star-shaped eye. The earliest of all primulas to bloom, and flowers for ten weeks. Several roots planted around a bowl, with a Craddock White in the centre, make a superb table decoration that remains in all its glory for several weeks. Magnificent under artificial light.

JOHN HAMMOND (3). A distinct large cherry-red bloom with large orange centre. A rare variety, and the colour is quite unique.

JULIAE (2). The most dwarf of all. The small dainty blooms are of a deep purple-blue flushed crimson. An ideal rock primrose.

JULIAE ALBA (3). Similar in habit to the better-known *Juliae*. A primrose well worth growing. The bloom is purest white and the constitution robust though dainty of habit.

JULIUS CAESAR (1). The first to flower, in Somerset about March 1st., and almost the last to remain in bloom. Free and compact, growing to a height of about five inches, the dark claret-red blooms have a small orange eye. The dark bronze foliage is most attractive. Plant with Craddock White or Harbinger.

KATHLEEN (2). A large rich navy-blue, flushed crimson and mauve, the blooms are held well above the foliage. Very prolific and long lasting.

KEITH (3). Another very rare variety having frilly petals and being of very dwarf habit. The colour is a delicate pale yellow.

KINLOUGH BEAUTY (4). An outstanding primrose having small dainty flowers of rich salmon-pink with a white candy stripe where the petals overlap. Of sturdy form the blooms are held well above the foliage. Ideal for window boxes.

LADY GREER (2). A superb Irish variety, the dainty polyanthus-type blooms are borne above the foliage. It is a pale yellow counterpart of Mrs. J. H. Wilson, but has a much longer flowering season. Looks really lovely in the early evening light. Makes an unusual but charming edging to a herbaceous border. Much admired by H.M. The Queen Mother at the Royal Horticultural Society's Show, March 1952.

LADY PRIMROSE (1). A bright yellow of dwarf polyanthus habit.

LAMBROOK YELLOW (2). A deep buttercup-yellow of polyanthus habit and very sturdy. From East Lambrook Manor.

LILAC BUNTY (2). This is a lilac-pink form of the rare Blue Bunty and equally lovely. Literally a mass of bloom in spring, with the characteristic yellow eye.

LILAC TIME (2). Of dwarf habit and of a delightful pale lilac-mauve, somewhere between Felicity and Iris Mainwaring.

LINGWOOD BEAUTY (3). A late variety, having bright cerise-crimson flowers with deep orange eye and bright green foliage.

LIZZIE GREEN (2). A unique new primrose having small star-like brick-red flowers, but unfortunately blooms for only a short period. Interesting.

MARTIN ARGLES (2). A lovely novelty having bloom of a deep claret purple with a bright orange and crimson centre. A most colourful primrose.

MAUREEN GENDERS (3). An outstanding primrose. The blooms are deep mahogany-crimson edged white, with a large pale yellow star-like centre. Free, though late in flowering, and has a long season. At its best in May.

MAUVE QUEEN (1). Very early indeed and excellent for bunching, the pure lilac-mauve blooms are held well above the foliage. Ideal for edging and window boxes.

Jack-in-the-Green
(*Photograph R. A. Malby & Co.*)

Hose-in-Hose or Duplex Primrose, Lady Lettice.
(Two-Year Plant)

MISS MASSEY (1). A lovely old variety now almost extinct. The habit is very dwarf and the blooms are of a rich bright ruby-red with the leaves a bright cucumber green. Mentioned by Walter Wright in his *Popular Garden Flowers*, published 1911.

MORTON HYBRID (4). Of very dwarf habit, the brilliant red blooms have a very large clear yellow centre. Very showy, but of not too easy culture!

MRS. MACGILLAVRY (2). Produces masses of rich violet-mauve flowers in March. Of sturdy constitution, a grand primrose.

MRS. FRANK NEAVE (3). A long-flowering, magenta-crimson variety, bearing a small dainty bloom with attractive bottle-green foliage.

MRS. PIRRIE (3). Of Scottish origin, this is a grand rock plant of dwarf habit; the rich mauve bloom is freely produced.

MRS J. H. WILSON (3). The sweetly perfumed tiny mauve blooms are held in great profusion above the foliage. An interesting variety but which is none too tolerant of strong sunshine.

PAM (2). Dainty crimson-purple, very free flowering over a long period. An ideal rock primula, having the smallest of all blooms.

PANTALOON (3). A very rare plant, the bright crimson flowers being shown off by a green ruff, flecked crimson and white, and remaining for many weeks in bloom.

PAULINE (3). A really lovely primrose, rather difficult to rear but well worth the effort. It is very dwarf, having a bloom of intense orange, flushed crimson and yellow. A Champernowne introduction, and really outstanding.

PINK BEAUTY (1), A new primrose, the blooms are of a pure shell-pink. Remains long in flower. Very dainty.

PINK BUNTY (3). Of a lovely rich pink colour with a very dwarf but sturdy habit.

PINK LADY GREER (3). As for Lady Greer (see page 48), but the colour is a delightful shell pink.

PRIMAVERA (3). Possibly the most striking variety. The flowers are of a brilliant orange-scarlet-crimson with no trace of mauve or magenta. The large orange eye makes it shine like a beacon.

PURPLE BEAUTY (3). A lovely primrose, having flowers of rich crimson, flushed mauve, and attractive pale green foliage.

PURPLE CUSHION (3). Rich claret and navy, like a super Wanda but not so tolerant of the sun. The foliage is unique, like that of a violet plant with stems of the leaves a brilliant red.

PURPLE SPLENDOUR (2). A lovely variety having large frilled crimson purple blooms with distinct pale yellow eye and pale green foliage.

RED CARPET (1). Raised by Dr. Douglas Smith. The plants are covered with a mass of tiny flowers of a most vivid scarlet-red shade.

RIVERSLEA (3). A very dwarf primrose and most uncommon, having very dark mauve flowers held well above the cushion-like foliage.

ROMEO (2). A superb variety, bearing huge vivid parma-violet blooms, flat like a pansy. Very prolific, early, and a strong grower. One of the best primroses in cultivation. Lovely when used as a carpet for yellow tulips.

ROSALIE (2). A rich pink which helped Dr. Smith to win the Ferne Cup for Primroses at the 1950 National Primula Society Show.

SINGLE GREEN (2). Very rare indeed, but so interesting that one plant should be in every collection.

SNOW-WHITE (1). A lovely new white recently introduced from the Continent and said to be very early.

SPRING DARLING (4). A unique colour of cherry-red flushed crimson and of dwarf polyanthus habit. This variety is a very strong grower.

SPRINGTIME (2). The colour of marshmallow purple, with blooms freely produced.

SUNSET GLOW (3). A magnificent novelty, almost a cross between Afterglow and Pauline, but possessing the slow-propagating attributes of both.

TAWNY PORT (3). An attractive, rare little primrose, very dwarf growing and the darkest of all, having maroon-green foliage and dainty dusk port-wine blooms. Of dwarf polyanthus habit. From the West of Ireland, and very long flowering.

THE SULTAN (2). This is a large *Juliae* hybrid having bloom of a rich brown shade. From the garden of that great primrose grower, William Goddard of British Columbia.

TINY TIM (3). Like an orange-red Pam and possibly has even smaller bloom. A perfect rockery primula.

TOPSY (2). Of polyanthus habit but of a completely new colour and formation. The blooms are wine-red with a biscuit-bronze centre.

TRIZONE (3). Found in a Devon garden; a most unusual variety having a dark red ring round the eye, with outer rings of purple and blue shades.

VERWANII, SIR BEDIVERE (4). A very rare primrose with crinkly bright green leaves and bears a large bronze-red flower with almost no eye.

VERONICA (3). A lovely variety of true *Juliae* habit. The flowers are steel-blue with a deep orange centre and are freely produced. A very unusual colour.

WANDA (2). This variety started the vogue of the *Juliae* primroses. One of the earliest to bloom and latest to finish, and the claret-red flowers thrive in full sun. Does well anywhere.

WANDA IMPROVED (2). From Scotland, and having a larger bloom than the original strain of Wanda.

WANDA'S RIVAL (2). Of true Wanda type but having flowers of a rich rosy-mauve colour. A grand primrose for edging. New and easy.

WENDY (2). Very pale pink, flushed mauve. A large bloom with frilled petals. Easy to propagate and very long-flowering indeed.

WILLIAM GENDERS (2). A grand variety similar in style to the lovely Kinlough Beauty (see page 48) but the colour is a pure violet-pink, candy-striped with white, making a most striking effect.

HOSE-IN-HOSE

ASHFORT (2). A tall-growing 'hose' of a brownish-red colour with pale green foliage.

BRIMSTONE (2). A new variety, being of true polyanthus habit on long stems and with large blooms like bells. The colour is rich sulphur-yellow.

BUFF BEAUTY (3). Of a delightful buff shade. Strong grower.

CANARY BIRD (1). A vivid pure yellow hose-in-hose freely produced. A rare primrose of delicate habit.

CERISE (2). Almost half-way between the red and mauve varieties.

DEEP PINK (3). Deeper in colour than the pink form. This is a really lovely primrose.

DUSKY MAID (3). Another new polyanthus hose, the colour is an attractive deep dusky rose-pink.

ERIN'S GEM (3). A lovely cream hose-in-hose from Ireland.

GOLDILOCKS (1). A tall-growing variety, with bloom of a rich golden yellow.

IRISH MOLLIE (2). A delightful rosy-mauve variety, very scarce and with not too strong a constitution. Also called Lady Molly.

LADY LETTICE (2). An amazing apricot hose-in-hose coming into a mass of bloom in late March and still in bloom in June. In flower again in autumn. Ideal for window boxes and for use as edging to a border. Lovely for cutting with Fair Maid.

LADY STEELE (4). A dwarf hose, similar in habit to Pam and Wanda hose-in-hose, but of the purest mauve, a colour much required in this section. Found in the gardens of Biddulph castle, Staffordshire.

OLD VIVID (3). Another old Irish introduction of a bright crimson shade and very free flowering. Of similar habit to Lady Lettice.

ORANGE PRINCE (3). Similar to Lady Lettice in habit, the bloom being primrose, flushed deep orange.

ORANGES AND LEMONS (2). A lovely old Irish variety with its primrose-yellow bloom shaded and splashed with orange.

PAM (HOSE-IN-HOSE) (3). As for Pam. A rare form. Tiny bloom.

PINK (HOSE-IN-HOSE) (2). A true pink, very lovely.

RUDDIGORE (3). Discovered in Co. Tyrone, a hose-in-hose of a beautiful clear crimson-red and of strong constitution. A very rare and fine primrose.

SCARLET (3). A very rare plant of intense beauty.

SPARKLER (2). A vivid crimson hose-in-hose, a lovely variety with no trace of magenta. The largest hose-in-hose and very strong growing.

THE CLOWN. (1). An unusual polyanthus hose-in-hose, the bright red flowers being mottled with white.

WANDA (HOSE-IN-HOSE) (2). As for Wanda. Now nearly extinct, but a strong grower and blooms profusely.

WINDLESTRAW (3). Of tall polyanthus habit, the large blooms are of a pale primrose-yellow colour, freely produced.

CHAPTER V

The Polyanthus: its Development for Cutting, Bedding aud Indoor Decoration

Not since the sixteenth century, when the cottager would beautify his tiny beamed room with an assortment of primrose and violets and other flowers we now call 'old-world', have we really appreciated the beauty of flowers indoors.

Flowers in the home, and this includes pot plants and miniature gardens too, are to-day as popular as flowers in the garden, and during springtime, before the daffodil shows its saffron face to the sun, the primrose (and later the polyanthus) turns its face towards the March winds almost begging to be taken indoors to the genial warmth of a sunny room. Not all the primroses we know to-day are suitable for cutting, nor is every strain of polyanthus, for raisers have concentrated on producing either a strain having a brilliantly coloured bloom on a long stem for the cut flower grower, or on raising a more compact plant that still has a large head of bloom on a short, sturdy stem, making for a most arresting bedding display in spring. The earliest polyanthus which were prized by the collector were the gold-laced types of half a century ago, and in 1909 the then National Auricula Society included seven classes in its annual show for Polyanthus, the gold-laced or 'edged' varieties being considered outstanding, and the black-ground varieties generally took the Premier Awards. At that time, three varieties were considered supreme: Tiny, which still retains its popularity with exhibitors of gold-laced polyanthus; Exile; and Mrs. Brownhill, named after the wife of Mr. Norman Brownhill, then Secretary of the National Auricula Society.

The Polyanthus

The requirements for a gold-laced polyanthus for exhibition were that the bloom should be circular, with a sharp gold edge, and have a round, clear centre. But though the gold-laced polyanthus was popular with the exhibitor, it never attained a firm place in the ordinary gardener's estimation. It was certainly a florists' flower, but its sombre background made its appeal very limited. As a bedding plant, too, it failed to satisfy Victorian standards of refined respectability, according to which, calceolarias and geraniums were almost the sole subjects for outdoor bedding, and the aspidistra was just the thing to shut out the sunlight from every front room window; the brazen scarlets and yellows of the polyanthus received, in such circumstances, little attention. A less obvious reason for the lack of popularity of the polyanthus and primrose was our forefathers' preoccupation (now difficult for us to appreciate in all its intensity) with the greenhouse. During the first Elizabethan age, Drake and others brought back many plants which were grown in the open in defiance of climate; the potato succeeded, the banana did not. As it became possible to make clear glass in larger panes, heated by flues instead of hot beds, the culture of 'exoticks' became a craze. These set a standard of gaudiness and put a premium upon the fashion for bedding plants that needed a greenhouse to grow them. The greenhouse in its glory was like a T.V. set; our gardeners were glued to it when it was new, and it took William Robinson and Gertrude Jekyll to initiate the return to less artificial aspects of horticulture.

These gay colours of the polyanthus were, however, known to mid-seventeenth century gardeners, for John Rea wrote:

'The red cowslip and oxlip are also of several sorts, all bearing many flowers on one stalk, in fashion like those of the field, but of several red colours, some deeper, others lighter, some bigger like oxlips.'

We are unable to find any mention of the polyanthus, as Rea knew it, before 1564, and it was not until a hundred years later that Miller tells us that, 'in some parts are many persons engaged in the culture of this flower', and that, 'they are so much esteemed as to sell for a guinea a root'.

Yet at that time, expensive as were the plants, a coloured engraving appearing in a book on gardening shows the polyanthus in a form that mid-twentieth-century gardeners would cast on to the compost heap. But during the latter years of the eighteenth century, the form of the polyanthus improved very noticeably, the colours were now more intense, and the individual blooms more refined; and in 1792, Maddock wrote that 'its present highly improved state is due to the effect of long and assiduous culture'.

A purely English flower, a hybrid of the primrose and the oxlip, the polyanthus had then not even reached Holland or any other part of the Continent, for during the entire eighteenth century we find no mention of it by any of the outstanding continental gardeners. It was left to that great gardener, Isaac Emmerton, to write on the polyanthus in 1816, and his small book listed thirty-six varieties of recent date. His book was immensely popular and quickly went into second and third editions.

But during the period 1650–1850, although the polyanthus was greatly prized as an exhibitor's flower or a valuable florists' flower, it possessed neither compactness of bloom for bedding purposes nor length of stem and brilliance of colour to commend it as a cut flower. It was left to Miss Gertrude Jekyll to foresee that one day the polyanthus would become one of our most popular flowers, and for years she devoted her spare time to raising whites of outstanding merit, particularly as to length of stem and size of bloom; and yellows in a wide variety of lovely shades. Even Gertrude Jekyll concentrated on the more conventional colours; the vermilions and blood reds and blues of the 1950's were still half a century away.

During Victorian days, as we have seen, the polyanthus took a back seat. Even in 1920 the report of the National Auricula Society noted: 'We are short of polyanthus growers', for the number of exhibitors had been sadly depleted by the war years. Not until a decade later was there a strain for either cutting or bedding that could compel the stranger to this flower to make a note of the plant for his next spring garden display. To-day, Gertrude Jekyll and those early enthusiasts would be amazed if they could behold the result of their pioneer efforts and see the superb colour range of the most sedate art shades, and the blazing scarlets and golds

and blues in almost every conceivable shade. No one, of recent
years, has done more for the polyanthus than the great gardening
firm of Blackmore and Langdon of Bath, and their Gold Medal
Award for their strain of polyanthus is the result of many years of
intensive work. The honour was well deserved. To-day the sales
of polyanthus must run into millions; it is said that on the Pacific
Coast of America alone, two million plants are sold annually.

In America, the Levys and the Chartres and McHenrys have followed in the steps of Miss Jekyll and given the world many arresting new colours and blooms of a habit and form never before
dreamed of.

For bedding, the whites and golden yellows of Miss Jekyll's
garden were most popular, but these were never genuinely popular
florists' colours, though the habit was good; it was not until the
blues and rusts and wine reds were introduced in suitable cut-
flower form that the polyanthus achieved its present authority.
About 1930 saw the growers of Cornwall and the West Country
plant this flower on a large commercial scale for the first time,
though for some years previously small plantings had been made
The new colour range and length of stem, and the fact that the
polyanthus lasted a full ten days in water with no dropping of its
petals to cause added work for the housewife, were features that
made for popularity; and with England becoming a nation of small
suburban homes and flats, the vogue for the polyanthus increased
out of all recognition. Here at last was the perfect springtime cut
flower, and the grower hastened to take it up. It was easy to grow,
quick to reproduce itself, and the cut bloom would travel well.
Again, it was a dual-purpose plant, the cut bloom selling well in
spring, and the plants in autumn and again from March to May
when in full bloom.

The polyanthus is propagated either from seed or by division
of the crowns, and both methods of reproduction may take place
at almost any period of the year, especially in the south-west. For
seed sowing, the most satisfactory time does appear to be early in
spring, in April, for the sun is then of sufficient power to ensure
quick germination. During summer and autumn the young plants
will be building up reserves of food to carry them through winter,

and they will give a delightful display of colour the following spring, just one year after sowing. Most gardeners use the young plants for bedding purposes as soon as the summer plants are removed in October, and this has generally been found to be the most suitable time for setting out the young plants. They will then enjoy a month of warm soil conditions to become thoroughly established before the winter frosts set in. For bedding, the young roots are set out about eight inches apart, and as they do not remain permanently in the beds but are lifted, split and re-planted into an odd corner soon after flowering, to make way for the summer bedding flowers once again, quite close planting may be done. The same considerations apply with the cut flower grower, who may be covering his plants with glass in early February and will wish to use his ground as economically as possible. Here, planting may be as close as five to six inches, the roots being split and replanted as soon as flowering has ended and the ground has been thoroughly cleaned and manured.

The polyanthus appears outstandingly beautiful when naturalized. In an orchard, or growing in 'open' woodland where the sunlight can easily filter between the trees, and which has been planted with daffodils and forget-me-nots, the richly coloured heads are at their best and the plants may be left undisturbed for several years.

Commercial growers of cut blooms now seem to agree that an open situation may not be the ideal setting for the plant but will ensure a more richly coloured bloom. But a position of full sunlight will be satisfactory only where an appreciable amount of humus can be incorporated in the soil. This is vitally important, for the roots must never at any time lack sufficient moisture and artificial watering may not always be possible; indeed, except in the private garden it will rarely be so. The polyanthus loves cow manure and a heavy mulch of horticultural peat which will gradually be incorporated in the soil by constant use of the hoe. Leaf mould, decayed seaweed and beech and oak leaves will be useful composts, for it is realized that gardeners in the second half of the twentieth century can no longer obtain unlimited supplies of farmyard manure. That all members of the primrose family must have moisture is proved by the fact that they grow profusely within ten miles of our coast-line, whether it be in Somerset, Devon or Cornwall; Sussex or Hampshire, or along the equally delightful coast-line of Norfolk and Suffolk; or even on the East Coast of Yorkshire, though here cold east winds delay the appearance of the eagerly-awaited blooms in spring.

Frances Bardswell, in her delightful book *Sea-coast Gardens*, published in 1908, mentions that a parcel of primroses she sent to a gardener in Central Germany failed to survive for more than two springs. This may indicate that the species do thrive best where they are in easy reach of water, Ireland being an excellent example of a region in which the polyanthus and primrose reproduce themselves to the limit of their power. Though the primrose family will grow almost anywhere, in chilly exposed positions and in a cold clay soil containing little humus, they do appreciate conditions as near as possible to those they enjoy in their natural state; and that means their heads in the sunshine and their roots in shade or in a soil where moisture is conserved to the maximum.

For those who have to grow their polyanthus in a heavy soil, a 4-oz. per square yard dressing of

> 2 parts hoof meal
> 4 parts bone meal
> 1 part sulphate of potash,

supplemented by horticultural peat, leaf mould or any of the humus-forming materials, will give excellent results. On light land, the bone meal should be replaced by two parts of superphosphate. But it must be said that neither polyanthus nor primroses will respond to artificial stimulants if the humus content of the soil is not considerable.

Length of stem is now a matter of course, the hybridists having achieved the long, thick stem so important to the cut-flower grower, and this quality of any strain must be given equal consideration with quality of bloom. Covering with cloches, or frames which are supported by timber, will tend to give an even larger stem. Where glass covering is being used it should be protected from strong winds by fastening down with rope or strong wire. Cloches are excellent means of covering plants in the open or plants in small pots which might be intended for exhibition. When Dutch lights are being used for covering, take care to see that not only are the plants set out to conform to the size of the lights, but that sufficient room is available between each row to facilitate the removal of the lights. The modern strains of poly-anthus are now so much in demand with the florist that there seems considerable scope for the use of glass covering for plants in all areas other than Devon and Cornwall, where glass is not really necessary.

When dividing the plants after flowering and re-planting, the soil should be carefully shaken from the roots so that not only will division be easier but it will also be possible to see whether any diseased or decayed root should be discarded. Any plants which show signs of yellow leaves are also unsuitable for replanting.

Polyanthus are more easily raised from seed than are primroses, for the seed is larger and nothing like so hard-skinned. There is, therefore, no need to provide the seed with periods of freezing to hasten germination. As the seed is expensive, as much as seventy shillings an ounce for the Exhibition strains, sowing should be done where the seedlings may be controlled, either in pans or boxes in a greenhouse or under the protection of frames, or into the open ground where they may be covered either by lights or cloches. Here the seed is thinly sown in drills four inches apart, the drills having first been lined with horticultural peat following the thorough preparation and cleaning of the ground.

The amateur will find that broadcasting the seed on to a clean piece of ground which has been given a dressing of coarse peat and sand will give a good germination if a sowing is made during the early weeks of summer and kept in a moist condition. It may be necessary to provide some protection from slugs by placing bran mixed with a proprietary preparation at regular intervals around the area. However, the amateur will be well advised to raise the quite expensive seeds under more controlled conditions. It is not every polyanthus lover who possesses a greenhouse or a cold frame or even a row of cloches, all of which are most valu-able in raising polyanthus seeds, but all of us can obtain a seed

pan or an old shallow box and procure a small quantity of John
Innes seed-sowing compost at the local seed store. A sheet of
clean glass will complete our requirements and the seed may be
raised under these conditions on the balcony of a flat for later use
in tubs or window boxes, or in a courtyard or even on a window-
sill, indeed in any position where there is sufficient sunlight for
germination. The seed should be kept just moist at all times but
over-watering, especially of the tiny seedlings, may cause them to
damp off. When the young plants are thoroughly established they
may have, and will appreciate, rather more water.

For bunching, several strains of the polyanthus are equally
suitable. Blackmore and Langdon's Gold Medal strain are useful
both for the florist and for bedding. Toogood's Excelsior is magnificent for cutting, and where particularly arresting colours are
required, the Brilliancy strain (believed to have been introduced
by Miss Davies of South Molton in Devon) is most valuable. Most
of the large seed houses supply a strain either for cutting or for
bedding, length of stem being the primary difference. Of recent
years William Lord of the Bardsey Nurseries, Leeds, has concentrated on the polyanthus for the florist, the brilliant colours and
delicately tinted art shades having replaced the gold-laced polyanthus of fifty years ago. There is a miniature strain of polyanthus
new to Great Britain and introduced from the Barnhaven Gardens
of Oregon. This resulted from a cross between the ordinary large-
flowered strains and the stalked-form *Juliae* primroses such as Lady
Greer and Fair Maid. This is a fairylike strain, ideal for window-
box display, and a most attractive cut flower, lasting over many
days in water.

The modern strains of polyanthus are ideal window-box subjects, and for this purpose two-year-old plants should be used.
These will provide a succession of flowering stems from early
April until well into May. Now that the painting of property is
being done more and more attractively, contrasts may be furnished by the polyanthus of to-day, as it may be obtained in
almost every conceivable colour. One of the most striking displays
of spring window-boxes we have seen was of the American Wine-
red polyanthus growing in boxes painted pale turquoise to match

the painted woodwork of the windows and shutters. This was offset by the whitewashed walls of the house. The clusters of deep wine-red polyanthus showed to magnificent advantage in the April sunshine.

For bedding, the polyanthus should be obtained in a strain specially bred for this purpose, one that is compact, growing to a height of no more than eight inches. The florets, too, should be large and close together, leaving no space between. The good bedding polyanthus should resemble a head of a cineraria plant, a mass of individual blooms touching but not overlapping and almost symmetrical in form. The stems should be stout and sturdy. The cut-flower polyanthus offers a long, wiry stem, with the florets smaller and more irregular in shape.

Modern strains of bedding polyanthus may be used in dozens of ways; for planting in long rows beneath a wall to form a polyanthus border, with a row of Primula Wanda as an edging; or for underplanting the taller-growing Darwin tulips, using the contrasting self colours. More and more are the self colours in demand, for these have now been fixed in the same way as Miss Jekyll fixed her whites and yellow shades. To-day we have geranium red and wine red, midnight blue and peach pink, apricot and ripe corn colour: that is, provided the finest strains are selected.

A lovely strain is the Giant Gold-Laced, having flowers an inch in diameter and each stem bearing about a dozen individual blooms. This strain was raised by Messrs Nutting & Sons, Limited, of Merstham. For range of colour, the Colessea strain introduced by Vaughan's Stores of West Jackson Boulevard, Chicago, U.S.A., is unsurpassed, for the colours include cream, mauve, lilac and crimson. This is possibly the finest strain for bedding for the flowers are almost two inches in diameter and are in trusses of twenty. The Festival Strain, raised by Mr. F. Read of Deopham, Wymondham, Norfolk, is extremely vigorous and free-flowering and includes apricot, bronze and pink in its colour range. Messrs. Michaud & Co., of the Alpenglow Gardens, British Columbia, have also introduced a very fine strain.

We should also like to put forward the Tudor, Jack-in-the-Green forms of the primrose as most attractive in the cut flower form. They take the polyanthus form with stems up to ten inches long, and are obtainable in every colour; though not yet possessing the extensive colour range we now associate with the modern polyanthus, they do possess a delightfully contrasting green ruff around the bloom. The Jacks are at their best when in the bunched form, especially when in water and mixed with polyanthus bloom or the long-stemmed *Juliae* primroses. The cut-flower specialist would be profitably advised to concentrate on this delightful section. They do not make such a large truss as the cut polyanthus, but the large green ruff prevents any appearance of sparseness. As with polyanthus, mixed bunches are most in demand, cut with as long a stem as possible, and containing a carefully chosen selection of colours. When bunching polyanthus, it is better to confine the colours to a tasteful grouping, for example, with the white and yellow colours, mix in red, orange and bronze. Where the blue polyanthus is being used, and there is now an attractive Oxford blue double strain on the market, then set this colour off with white, cream or pale yellow shades. If dark crimson or orange is used with blue, the colours tend to clash.

Always pick polyanthus and primroses in the early morning, while the dew is still on the plants, and the grower interested in the sale of cut blooms should, after bunching with a rubber band, stand his flowers in bowls of cold water for at least two hours before packing in the 'anemone'-sized boxes, and despatching to market. The bloom should be cut the moment it has opened, for at this stage it will remain fresh for travelling, and in water, for a considerable time.

As the earliest flowering stems fade away, to prolong the season of flowering they should be cut off to prevent the plant diverting its energies to the formation of seed rather than to additional flowers. If it is the intention to save one's own seed for sowing the following spring, then those flower heads which may have given evidence of some outstanding colour or size should be marked with a small wooden label and the seed should be allowed to form and ripen. But too many dead flowers allowed to remain in a bed will only cause an untidy appearance, and later bloom will suffer as a result.

The Polyanthus

Plants of polyanthus and all primroses should be lifted in damp weather and should be packed in damp moss if they are to go through the post. The commercial grower will find that sales of primrose plants reach their peak during April and May whilst the plants are in full bloom, when they should be railed in strong boxes in an upright position so that the bloom is in no way damaged. Name with a small wooden label and spread a layer of damp moss at the bottom of the box. Spray the bloom before despatching and the plants should arrive at their destination in perfect condition. This procedure should not only be carried out by the commercial grower, but also by the amateur who may wish to exchange plants with friends or send small numbers away as gifts.

While on the subject of polyanthus and primroses as cut flowers, a word must be said about some of the other types and varieties which lend themselves to cutting. Most of the doubles are excellent when cut and bunched with primrose leaves or even with ivy leaves. Among the best are double white *Alba plena*, Marie Crousse and Burgundy. These are excellent varieties for cloching in February. Equally attractive is the single Mauve Queen, the earliest of all primroses to bloom in spring, the blooms of pale mauve being carried on long wiry stems. For later cutting, those two long-stemmed varieties, Fair Maid, orange-rust with a vivid double yellow centre, and Lady Greer, with its fairylike pale yellow heads of bloom, should prove highly popular with florists if marketed in a fresh condition. During the last week of April, there is nothing more enchanting in the home than these two varieties in mugs or bowls of darkened glass, and both carry the delicate primrose perfume. Another lovely table decoration is achieved by mixing the charming creamy-apricot hose-in-hose variety, Lady Lettice, with a few stems of the grape hyacinth, *Muscari*, Heavenly Blue. Lady Greer mixed with Kinlough Beauty, and the blue strain or the red, Joan Schofield mixed with the common yellow primrose, are all charming floral combinations.

In the Asiatic section, there are many varieties that make a most charming display in the home. Try the deep purple heads of *Primula denticulata*, Hay's Variety with the exquisitely perfumed

Modern Polyanthus (Blackmore & Langdon strain) exhibited at Royal Horticultural Society Show, May 1950, and awarded a Gold Medal

(Photograph Blackmore & Langdon)

Polyanthus in a perfect setting

yellow bells of *Primula Sikkimensis* for early May decoration. Or the delicate pinks and apricots of *Primula pulverulenta*, Bartley Strain, originating from the late Mr. Dalrymple's Nursery at Southampton; or the vivid tangerine, *Cockburniana*, for later in May, or the yellow bells of *Primula Florindae* for late June decoration. For cutting, many of the primulas make most original and interesting house decorations from March to June, a most difficult period for cut blooms, when only Iris, Pyrethrums and the later-flowering tulips are available to the housewife.

The cowslip hybrids of recent introduction make a most delightful display in early summer. They produce heads of every conceivable colour on stems about fifteen inches tall, and not only are they a most attractive garden plant when planted in groups, but are ideal for cutting. From a good strain of seed, they will germinate readily, in exactly the same way as polyanthus. These lovely plants deserve to be more widely grown, and all who have seen them massed in the garden of a house in Bridgwater, Somerset, could not fail to purchase a packet with their next seed order.

CHAPTER VI

Double Primroses

PART I—1597 TO 1875

During the reign of Elizabeth I Gerard, writing in 1597 of the primrose family, mentions that 'our garden Double Primrose, of all the rest is of the greatest beautie'. This is the first reference to this plant that we know, although Gerard's wording does not suggest that there was any novelty about it. He has been accused of copying much of Clusius's *Rariorum Plantarum Historia* (written in the middle of the sixteenth century), but this is not the case when he deals with double primroses, for there is no mention of these plants in that work.

Twenty years later, in 1629, Parkinson, in his *Paradisi in Sole*, gives us this description of what he calls 'the ordinary double primrose': 'The leaves of this primrose are very large and like unto the single kind, but somewhat larger, because it groweth in gardens: the flowers do stand every one severally upon slender long footstalks, as the single kind doth, in greenish huskes of a pale yellow colour, like unto the field primrose, but very thicke and double, and of the same sweet scent with them.'

This is a very clear description not only of the double primrose of the seventeenth century but also of the plant to-day. It is interesting to notice that, whereas Parkinson describes the double sulphur-coloured primrose as 'ordinary', it is a double white that is illustrated in Gerard's *Herbal*. Oddly enough, in the first edition of the latter it is shown as a polyanthus but is altered to a true primrose in the third.

Double Primroses

There is significance in the fact that the writers of the seventeenth and eighteenth centuries did not produce long or involved accounts of double primroses. From the tone of what they wrote, it seems certain that they accepted them as a matter of course. They give one the impression of having a genuine and enthusiastic affection for them, of wanting them in their gardens and of knowing that they could have them too. They were plants that had always been there, an accepted part of the garden. Thus, John Rea in his *Flora* of 1665:

'The Common Double Garden Primrose is so well known that it is sufficient onely to name it, but were it not so common in every Country-woman's Garden, it would be more respected, for indeed it is a sweet and dainty double flower and the chiefest of all our English Kinds.' This is the genuine feeling of an enthusiast which is echoed a hundred years later by Hanbury in his *Gardening* (1770):

'A sufficient number of roots of these three sorts (yellow, white and crimson) to form a large bed, all planted together, will have a most enchanting look.'

In the *Botanical Magazine* for 1794 Curtis, again with enthusiasm, suggests a definite use for double primroses.

'These several varieties of Primrose are admirably adapted to the decoration of the shrubbery, plantations or even the north side of rock-work.'

As the nineteenth century is reached, we find more and more pages devoted to the cultivation of polyanthus and fewer and shorter accounts of double primroses. If the wealth of detailed instructions means anything, gardeners' ideas have undergone a very revolutionary change since then, on the subject of polyanthus and double primroses, for writers in the first three quarters of the nineteenth century do little more than report a list of colours of the latter. Occasionally there is an article that is longer, but only because it contains a large number of not very relevant pieces of poetry. It must be remembered that the nineteenth century saw the birth of many gardening magazines which, in their turn, offered wide scope to people to record their views and experiences. The letters and articles seem to have been evoked by a competitive instinct rather than an earnest desire to add to the existing knowledge of these plants, but they are of interest to-day as giving proof of the wide range of colours that existed then.

'Isobella', writing in the *Floricultural Cabinet* for 1846, offers us a picture of more interest than can be derived from a bare recital of a number of varieties of double primroses: 'This very lovely little flower, the double primrose, ranks high in my estimation and the following kinds form my present collection—double crimson, white, purple, straw colour, rose, deep yellow, pink, buff, lilac and red, each of them being very double and distinct. I am fully assured if the entire of them were seen when in bloom in my flower garden, as presented to view from the breakfast-table, in a sunny spring morning, they would not fail to please every lover of flowers.'

From all the sources that we have read from Gerard to 1875 we have compiled the following list of colours and we would repeat that, except for the one case of the illustration in the first edition of Gerard's *Herbal*, we have seen no suggestion that a single variety was anything but a true primrose as opposed to a polyanthus.

Blush	Dark Purple	Purple
Bright Crimson	Deep Crimson	Rose
Buff	Deep Yellow	Salmon Pink
Carmine	Dingy	Straw
Copper	Flesh	Sulphur
Cream	Green	Violet
Crimson	Lilac	White
Crimson Purple	Pink	Yellow

It is a tremendous list which modern polyanthus could not even approach, for we have never seen mention of the colour green for the latter. Clearly there can be no description of individual coloured varieties. They were just all double primroses. It is interesting to note that blue is not included in the list. Elsewhere in this book there is an account of the origin of blue primroses, a coloured form which is, presumably, very much man-made.

Now from this period of nearly three hundred years two important facts emerge. First, no names (as opposed to colours) are mentioned. One sees from time to time in present-day accounts that such and such a named variety (Mme. Pompadour or Arthur Du Moulin are the usual examples) is 'very old', and attempts are made to produce a sort of pedigree, with reasons why the name goes back well into this particular period. So also by the use of a capital letter at the beginning of a word, a colour has become a proper name. 'Dingy' is given as a colour by Loudon in 1830 and the word is used to describe a colour but not as a name. Again, in consecutive editions of a catalogue, outside this period but published at the end of the nineteenth century, one may find 'burgundy' used as a colour designation, while in the next edition the same word is printed beginning with a capital letter, and it thus becomes a proper name. But there is no real evidence that, in fact, names existed before 1875. Writers like 'Isobella' would most certainly have used names if they had existed, a not unreasonable supposition if one knows that about half her article consisted of poetical quotations from Keats, Browne, Wordsworth, Ben Jonson, Herrick and John Clare. It is quite likely that her double crimson was the same plant as the present-day Mme. Pompadour, but she did not call it by name. Yet hers was a time when names abounded. Eight years earlier Mc'Intosh published a list of four hundred and forty-seven different named ranunculus and sixty-nine named varieties of polyanthus, yet not one of these names survives to-day in these plants. It is not to be supposed that no one gave his plants names. That has happened always, although any names that were given to double primroses in this period could only have been local or sentimental, for they did not become universal.

We now come, in this period, to new creations.

Creating New Varieties

Miller, that famous eighteenth-century author of the *Gardener's Dictionary* which was republished in many editions even well into Victorian times, wrote, ' There are several varieties of this (double primrose) which have been accidentally obtained, as the paper-white primrose with single and double flowers, the crimson primrose with double flowers, the red primrose with single and double flowers, these have but one flower upon a foot stalk.'

Double Primroses

The important word in this quotation is 'accidentally'. In our Foreword we quoted John Hill as writing that 'from favouring circumstances and a luxuriance in Nature, it has been found in the fields'. Hanbury, in 1759, wrote a book entitled *A Method of Producing Double Flowers from Single*, but in it makes no mention of double primroses. Yet in his *Gardening* he writes of them at some length and disagrees emphatically with Miller in the latter's ideas about their cultivation. Here, then, is a man who, one might expect, would have dealt with the subject of creating new varieties of double primroses but does not do so. Either he and his contemporaries did not know, or else 'accidental' methods provided them with all the varieties that they wanted. This is, admittedly, an unsatisfactory argument, but in the absence of positive evidence no other conclusion can be reached.

Culture

In dealing with this subject we propose to make a number of quotations in chronological order and reserve comment until the end.

1731. (Miller). 'They delight in a strong soil but will grow in almost any sort of earth provided they have a shady situation.'

1758. (Hill). 'The Common Gardener needs no other Instructions on this head than to part the Roots at Autumn, and plant them in fresh Pasture Ground, enriched by the addition of a little Wood-Pile earth and Cow-dung. Here they will keep their Beauty and demand from him very little Care.'

1770. (Hanbury). '. . . a shady border as rich as possible, fresh, loose, rich mould.'

1794. (Curtis). 'They delight to grow in a stiff loam, a moist and somewhat shady situation. So planted they thrive admirably, the double succeeding almost as well as the single. Every second or third year their roots should be divided which may be done either in spring or autumn. They may be cultivated also in pots for the convenience of removing them when in bloom.'

1838. (Mc'Intosh)'. 'They grow and flower luxuriously in a mixture of rich loam and leaf mould, with a small proportion of peat.'

1854. (*Florist and Pomologist*). 'After flowering they should be taken up, roots divided, and planted in a moist shady situation. Transplant in autumn if possible.'

1874. (*Florist and Pomologist*). 'During the summer months a little shade during the heat of the day, but especially a deeply-stirred and moderately rich soil in which the roots can descend freely in search of moisture. With the common kinds, white or lilac, I find no difficulty in growing them in the open ground exposed to the full glare of the sun. How far in a deep clayey loam such as the soil here the choicer kinds would thrive under the same conditions, remains to be seen.'

Although these quotations cover a long period of time, they all possess a marked similarity. From them may be collected certain pointers which amount to the principles for growing double primroses so far as the site and soil are concerned—the provision of a shady situation and rich soil. If the prospect of finding a 'little Wood-Pile earth' is a little daunting, it is, after all, not much different from leaf mould. And there are no other curious ingredients in any of the recipes.

In two of the quotations, that of Curtis and the *Florist and Pomologist* of 1854, there are instructions for propagation. Miller states that the best time to transplant is at Michaelmas, but whether he refers to propagating double primroses or planting them out in their spring site is not clear.

Uses

If only to gain some picture of the composition of formal flower beds—and, again, we would stress that the age of formality continued almost up to the end of this period—we include certain quotations which mention the uses made of double primroses in gardens. In Beck's *Florist* for 1849 there is an article on 'Spring Flowers'. Of double primroses, it says: 'If the flower beds are small they may be planted in masses of different colours with good effect; but if large, they look better regularly mixed, or the centre of the bed may be filled with one colour and the margin with another.' A more elaborate arrangement in the spring gardens at Belvoir is described in the *Villa Gardener* of 1873: 'A bed made up of a central cluster of *Erica Sordida*, edged with *Andromeda Tetragona*, followed by dwarf wallflower and double lilac primroses . . . a mass of *Saxifraga cordifolia*, white and pink hyacinths, oxlip, pansy, bright yellow primroses and double white primroses . . . a centre of *Scilla trifolia*, Alpine auricula, double primroses, lilac crimson and white.'

Another garden described in 1851 consisted of nineteen beds 'cut out in a uniform figure on the lawn' and the centre consisting of roses edged with double primroses.

The impression left from even these few quotations—and there are many others in the same style—is that double primroses must have been looked on as reliable bedding-out plants. If in those days they were as difficult to cultivate as one is led to believe that they are to-day, no one, and particularly in that age of formality, would have used them for the purpose. At best they would have been given a place in Curtis's 'shrubbery, plantations or even the north side of rock-work'.

There were other ways of featuring the flowers, one of which is described in the *Villa Gardener* of 1872: 'The Double White English Primrose is particularly valuable as a window plant as it does not suffer so much for the want of full light as some plants do. Then the flowers are so fragrant; for my taste the violet is not more grateful than the smell of a good Primrose. As a bouquet flower it is equal to the best. The pure white flowers are always welcome, and then they already have somewhat long stems. One after another, too, flowers come into quick succession. It is, moreover, a plant of very easy culture.'

And, to return to 'Isobella': 'About the latter end of September they should be carefully taken up, and potted into wide shallow pots of sufficient size not to cramp the roots, using the compost already recommended. I have a quantity of pots, whilst the plants are in bloom, in my sitting room, where they flourish beautifully, and give a sweet cheerfulness to it.'

Double Primroses

But let us hasten to add that Isobella is a most dangerous authority to quote, for it is easy enough for anyone to read the rest of her article. If she was as pernickety with her primroses as she leads one to believe in the course of her article, then it is almost a miracle that she ever had anything to look at from her sitting-room window. Nevertheless she was of her time, and doubtless a local toast. Her use of double primroses as pot plants is a good one, but the two things to avoid are taking them indoors too early and giving them too much heat. They should be taken in when the first flowers are beginning to burst from the bud, and the plants must be kept as cool as possible.

It seems quite clear to us that, through all this long period, double primroses were much-loved plants, not only for their own beauty but also for their mass effect and ease of cultivation. One hears often enough to-day that, in the past, 'they' had more time. It would be more accurate to say that they may have had fewer diverse interests with which to occupy their time, for there were still only twenty-four hours in the day, then as now. We know from our own practical experience how great a difference there may be between plants of double primroses grown casually and those which have been grown in conditions that approximate to those that were normal during the period with which this chapter deals. This seems to us to be the crux of the whole problem, which can be summed up by saying that if one wants to grow double primroses at all one must just get back to the conditions of soil and situation prevailing in the days when they were common-place plants. We would conclude this chapter by quoting William Robinson in the *English Flower Garden*: 'No sweeter or prettier flowers ever warmed into beauty under a northern sun than their richly and delicately-tinted little rosettes . . . Double Primroses well grown, and the same kinds barely existing, are such different objects, that nobody will grudge them the trifling attention necessary to their perfect development.'

CHAPTER VII

Double Primroses

PART II—1875 TO 1953

I t is in this chapter that we propose to show what has happened between the days of plenty and the present time when, we believe, it would be very hard to find anyone who could supply a hundred plants of any except two or three varieties, or indeed anyone who possessed more than about a dozen varieties altogether. The history of the last seventy-five years must be surveyed as two main themes—the first dealing with the disappearance of practically all of the twenty-four coloured varieties of double primroses listed in the last chapter, and the second with the arrival of the named varieties dealt with in Chapter IX.

During the last twenty-five years of the nineteenth century the number of hardy primula species introduced into this country, and made generally available, increased very considerably. With that increase in number came also a quickening interest and enthusiasm. For example, at the Primula Conference of 1886 there was no mention made at all of double primroses in the proceedings or in the various papers read. They were only admitted in one of the twenty-two competitive classes and in this class there were only two entries. Only one nurseryman included any in his exhibit. Florists' auriculas naturally took the lion's share at this conference, but hardy primulas were also plentiful. The story of the florists' auriculas is well known, of the enthusiasm that these plants inspired in men of all social classes, particularly in the north of England, of the lengthy instructions regarding their cultivation that appeared in gardening papers, and of the number of

74

letters that were also published about them. Thus a great number
of people could not have failed to be aware of them even if all did
not grow them themselves. Doubtless the growing of a florist's
auricula was too fiddling a process to appeal to a great many, so
that the alpine auriculas and their hybrids, and the other primula
species, offered a more attractive proposition which had the added
zest of novelty. Double primroses had always been there. There
was no novelty about them. The facts that have so far been recorded, and any deductions that may be made from them, have,
however, only a limited value because of the comparatively small
number of people to whom they applied. Furthermore most of
these folk would have been in sufficiently affluent circumstances
to have been able to afford the new plants that were becoming
available.

The next factor is that lack of interest. Quotations have frequently been made from *The Garden*, and there are many more
extracts that have been omitted. It was a paper that seemed to
have an interest in double primroses. Yet mention of them after
1913 occurs on an average only about once in every two years. In
the *Gardener's Chronicle*, for example, there is not one reference
from 1894 until Alex Dean wrote in 1910, with regard to a
suggestion to determine the origin of polyanthus, 'Of greater
interest would be an enquiry as to the origin of the race of double
garden primroses with which we are so familiar and of which we
still have some ten or twelve distinct varieties. (He had presumably
not come across the work of Cocker or Murray Thomson at the
time.) It is believed that practically every one of the doubles in
commerce came to us from the Continent. In any case I know of no
record of their origin.'

But add to this a great deal of pessimism, lack of any sort of
encouragement, directions for their culture so involved as to make
it just not worth the trouble, and that sums up the contribution
made by the gardening press in the last years of the century. It is
a very material reason for a lack of interest. In a 'Questions and
Answers' feature in one paper, this is written of double primroses:
'These are delicate in constitution and when not protected, are
apt to die off during winter, wet and cold being prejudicial to

them.' As most winters are both wet and cold, this contribution is
not too helpful. It is not even accurate as, in our experience, cold
has no effect on double primroses. Again, a staff writer, replying
to a question about how to grow double primroses, after giving
a most involved soil mixture, goes on to say that 'cowdung should
be buried nine inches deep, and the bed should be sunk, the aim
being to retain a humid, still atmosphere. To attain this the bed
should be surrounded with osier hurdles, padded with bracken,
and freely syringed in dry periods.' This is enough to frighten the
most enthusiastic.

For a different reason an extract from an article by Richard
Dean in the *Gardener's Chronicle* of 1879 is significant: 'The white,
lilac and yellow double primroses are much grown round London
for market purposes. They are planted out in beds between cur-
rant and gooseberry bushes and underneath the boughs of standard
apple, pear and plum trees. Hundreds of these plants are purchased
every spring and planted out in an unskilful manner in improper
soil where they soon die. It is then said, that they are of delicate
constitution, which is not true, the main reason of decay being
that they are not put into the kind of soil in which there is reasonable hope of success.' In contemporary advertisements the cost of
these plants varied from 4d. to 6d. apiece and they were offered,
as Dean suggests, as bedding plants. This must have gone on for
some time for a writer in *Gardening Illustrated* in 1886 suggests
that 'their effectiveness is often the cause of their decay owing to
the prominent exposed positions accorded them in the flower
garden'. If one thinks of the limited methods of propagation of
double primroses it can be clearly appreciated that where nurserymen oversold their stock and then resorted to some other type of
bedding plant to maintain their income and trade, the former
would very quickly die out in that district. Even more so would
this be the case if, as we are told, they were planted in positions
without thought as to how they would continue to grow in them.
Indeed, to the man who had to make his living out of providing
plants to the ever-increasing number of town dwellers, there must
have been many plants more commercially attractive than double
primroses. Once they had practically disappeared there was no

getting them back unless some nurseryman cared to specialize in them, to exhibit them, and, in fact, to re-introduce them deliberately to the public.

We have found no reference, towards the end of the century, to the existence of double primroses in cottage gardens. We believe that they survived there longer than elsewhere if only because of the reputed conservatism of country people. But the need to grow as much food as possible during the first World War must have removed a great many. Since then, all sorts of plants have been offered in every market town in the country for cottage folk to buy, various weekly papers are packed with advertisements, and seeds and bulbs are offered in ever more attractive packets. Why should country people return to a plant that only the oldest of them once knew, and which, in any event, has been nearly un-obtainable for a long time?

Miss Gertrude Jekyll, in a paper which she read at the Primula Conference of 1913, used these words: 'In these days when good hardy flowers are so much prized and so well used, it is difficult to account for the general neglect of the fine old double primroses.' She did not attempt to account for it, and left the subject there. A remark such as that, even from so famous a person, together with the very occasional short letters to a gardening paper, could scarcely suffice to revive an enthusiasm. Indeed, until about 1910, any answers that were given to such letters seem to have come from one or the other of the two Dean brothers, and the effect of Alex Dean's replies was to annoy rather than to persuade.

It is very noticeable in the various catalogues that have been examined that the number of varieties of double primroses offered becomes steadily less from the beginning of the present century to the outbreak of the first World War. Some firms which had included up to a dozen or more varieties were listing none in their catalogues by 1910.

It must be obvious enough, after a moment's reflection, that no nursery could possibly stock everything or necessarily keep more than a token stock of many of the plants mentioned in its cata-logue. Furthermore, plants for which there was no reasonable demand would be discarded. A nursery must, therefore, have its own sources from which it can buy in additional material when required. In the case of double primroses, Ireland and Scotland provided those sources. No one would deny that primroses grow excellently in certain parts of both countries (they probably grow equally well in parts of England) and the plants sent over, and then distributed by nurseries in England, must have been of fine quality. They were grown in the rectories, farms and larger houses. But gradually times have changed. Houses and their gardens were destroyed; their occupants have died or left, so that now, we believe, it would be nearly as hard to find double primroses in either country as it is to find them in England. Only very recently Major Taylor received a letter in which the writer said that he had gone back to have a look at his old home, where double primroses used to grow abundantly, only to find that the garden was a builder's yard. One nurseryman of our acquaintance used to get excellent double primroses in wide variety from a lady in Ireland. Recently she died and he wrote to the people who inherited the house to ask them to continue to supply him. They replied that they were not in the least interested in double primroses, could not tell one variety from another, and refused his offer to go over to Ireland and buy whatever he could find. If the nurseryman's source of supply ceases to exist his activity as a distributor ceases also, and, with it, the possibility of keeping both interest and enthusiasm alive. So the plants become more rare, for they will not keep alive for ever without attention.

We have had an unfortunate experience of this nature ourselves. We knew a very small nursery in Surrey where, up to the outbreak of the last war, there was a grand bed of one of the red double primroses. Duty took us past the gate four years later. The nursery had been abandoned and there were no primroses.

So these trivial reasons for the disappearance of double primroses can be recorded, and there may well be many more. Those we have traced are, briefly, incorrect treatment and use; lack of interest in the gardening press; diminishing commercial attraction and the arrival of many largely advertised and cheap plants; reduction, to the point of elimination, of sources of supply in Scotland and Ireland. Yet none of these proves that double prim-

roses cannot be grown or, indeed, are even difficult to grow. It
has been said that they cannot be grown in the south of England,
yet Waterers of Knaphill grew them admirably, Richard Dean outside London; and in Exmouth, Exeter, Ashtead, Broxbourne, and
many other places they were grown commercially until interest in
them died out. In so far as the coloured, and un-named, varieties
of double primroses are concerned, the truth is that they have died
out through lack of interest and through neglect, which may be
the same thing, but there is no case for assuming that they died
because they were difficult to grow.

We now pass to the second part of the history of the last
seventy-five years—the introduction of named varieties. Now the
ordinary generative parts of a flower have, in the case of double
primroses, been turned into what may be loosely called 'petals'.
There is, therefore, no pollen to be obtained from most varieties
or, if any at all, very little indeed. By some process of nature, seeds
from an ordinary single primrose have produced plants which
have included one which ultimately throws double flowers. That
this does happen is quite clear, not only from the fact that double
primroses can be found wild, but that the old writers have recorded it and that we have, ourselves, found double primroses and
have recorded the details in the next chapter. But the accident of
a double flower is not the only thing that may happen. There are
many other variations. First, there is the ordinary Jack-in-the-
Green primrose as described in Chapter IV, whose calyx appears
as a leafy growth immediately beneath the flower, varying in
length according to the variety. In our experience, in the case of
the primrose-coloured Jack-in-the-Green, it is short and does not
extend beyond the petals of the flower itself, whereas in other
colours it is much more distinct and appears as a distinct leafy
collar. There is a certain white variety in which it is very long and
narrow and in which the flowers themselves are sometimes curi-
ously distorted. Second, there is the variation known as 'Jackanapes', in which the enlarged calyx, instead of being uniformly
green, contains streaks of the same colour as the flower. When the
flower dies this has the effect of appearing as another flower remaining. Third, Jackanapes-on-Horseback goes one better than

the last, for while the calyx is much the same, a number of single-flowered pedicels appear from it instead of single flowers only. Fourth, Galligaskins have a much more prominently developed calyx than the Jack-in-the-Green with, in addition, a crisped or curled effect both in the petals of the flowers and in the edges of large foliaceous blades. Fifth, there are the hose-in-hose primroses (and polyanthus) in which one flower appears out of the centre of another—a duplex effect—in some varieties being very distinct, whereas in other the lower flowers lie close up to the upper one. Sixth, Pantaloons are hose-in-hose primroses but with the Jack-in-the-Green characteristic of the calyx forming a collar of apparent leaves below the flowers. Lastly, we have observed, and have also been sent, a double primrose with this same Jack-in-the-Green characteristic, although we have never seen mention of this in any old account. Here, then, are seven varieties of primrose—and with the ordinary double primrose, eight—which may arise from the seed of a single primrose. Unhappily, what does arise from all this as well is that it is so far quite impossible to control the results of trying to raise double primroses from seed. Dr. Amsler, writing about the new double, Delmonden Mauve, said, 'I got three dozen seedlings. Most were of a nasty colour, several were ose-in-hose or jack-in-the-box [*sic*]. I threw these away as I did not then know that some people cherished these oddities.'

In the light of what has been written, no possible gaurantee can be given, either, that any double primroses will appear at all from seed, although it is fairly likely that some will do so; or that such double primroses as do appear will be of any value.

In the Royal Horticultural Society's *Journal* of 1911 we read the following description of how Messrs. Cocker of Aberdeen raised the strain which they ultimately called Bon Accord double polyantha primroses: 'Messrs. Cocker of Aberdeen sent a large number of flowers of double polyanthus and primroses which they had raised from seed. The colours ranged from primrose-yellow through white to purplish blue shades but were not, as a rule, very bright. They were raised by crossing the Wisley blue primrose with the well-known *Polyanthus platypetala plena*. In the second and third

Double Primrose, Arthur du Moulin

(Photograph R. A. Malby & Co.)

generations numerous double-flowered forms had appeared in a wide range of colours.'

Now *platypetala plena*, or as it is (possibly incorrectly) known now, Arthur Du Moulin was first mentioned in English gardening literature in 1879, although it is found in a Belgian catalogue of 1871, which suggests that it came from the Continent. 'Recently there has been introduced to English gardens from the Continent a pretty pale mauve-coloured double primrose under the name of Arthur Dumoulins. This throws up blossoms on single stems and also in a scape; it is very bright and effective and has a glaucous dark green foliage, quite distinct in character.' (R. Dean in the *Gardener's Chronicle*.) It is one of the double primroses that fairly readily gives pollen, and was available when the Cockers started their experiments; but, and this is a very significant point, it is strictly speaking a polyanthus. Prince Silverwings, another polyanthus to give pollen, was a later introduction, and we have found no nineteenth-century reference to its being used as a pollen parent. We believe, therefore, that the polyanthus 'blood' now commonly found in most varieties points, firstly, to *platypetala plena* being the original ancestor, and, secondly, to the fact that all named varieties that have a polyanthus tendency must have originated since its introduction.

In the *Gardener's Chronicle* for 1910, Alex Dean wrote: 'I believe practically every one of the doubles in commerce came to us from the Continent. In any case I know of no record of their origin here.' If the important words in that quotation are 'in commerce', there might be a modicum of truth in it only because very few varieties were being offered at that date, but we believe that we have shown that, in general, Dean's belief is inaccurate. The truth is that men like the Cockers and Murray Thomson were clever and enthusiastic hybridists who, between them, raised a great number of varieties, only a relatively small proportion of which were ever distributed on a commercial scale. All may have been good in their various ways, and there are certain passages in gardening papers which bear this out, but we are forced back to the general indifference to double primroses to find cause why, to-day, so few of those varieties can be found. Of later years and, in a way, working with the hybridists because they all knew each other and passed their plants round, were a few enthusiastic growers and collectors. The Rev. P. H. Mules, Dr. McWatt who was, himself, something of a hybridist but not, we believe, very successful, the Rev. Mr. Murdoch, the Rev. Mr. McMurtrie and the Misses Cadell are a few names that come to mind, and these growers were not afraid of their enthusiasm. In Robinson's *English Flower Garden* there is a long and interesting quotation from an account that the Rev. Mr. Mules wrote to *The Field*; and in *Gardening Illustrated* for 1914 we read that 'there is a complete collection of the old double primroses in the garden of Dr. McWatt'; but unfortunately, no mention is made of any variety except French Grey.

It has been said that amateur gardeners of great ability have made a bigger contribution to gardens than the professional growers; and within the dangerous limits of generalization, there may be a good deal of truth. It would scarcely be an economic proposition today for a nurseryman to attempt to raise new varieties of double primroses from seed, for his attempts might continue for a number of years without any marked success and, in the end, he would be faced with the interval of time necessary to work up a commercial stock. But it does offer an intriguing field for the keen and skilful amateur. If, however, there is such a one who has the good fortune to raise a fine new variety let it be said, as a summary to this chapter—and it cannot too often be said—that the future of that plant will depend, as will the future of all double primroses, on employing the time-honoured methods of gardening. No matter how these methods may be described, or what technical or refined phrases may be used, they all boil down to the countryman's 'bags o' muck'.

To conclude this chapter: the great re-awakening of interest in both double and single primroses observed during the Coronation year is worthy of note. It is yet too early to give our opinion as to why this has come about. That these lovely flowers were truly characteristic of the Tudor Elizabethan era, and so are now in vogue once again, may be the primary cause of the tremendous interest. It may be that the articles of the authors which have

Double Primroses

appeared in *Popular Gardening, Gardening Illustrated* and other sections of the gardening press have created new interest. During the late summer of 1953 *The Field* published a considerable correspondence on the subject of quaint primroses, and several sources of supply were disclosed, all pointing to this revival of interest. So great now is the demand for these plants that for the first time for half a century, several nurseries are now concentrating entirely on them, yet they are still not able to satisfy the huge demand. For the authors this is the most encouraging news since the advent of the Bon Accords more than fifty years ago. To the modern gardener, the showing and descriptions of these lovely plants are opening up new interest; no longer is Primula Wanda the only variety known to many. It is to be hoped that this small book will create more and more enthusiasts.

CHAPTER VIII

Double Primroses

PART III—PERSONAL EXPERIENCE
(by Major H. C. Taylor)

Just to make certain that the right target is chosen for criticism or argument, this chapter will be written in the first person singular. Where I use the word 'we', I refer to my son, Peter, and myself.

Not so long ago I read a book, fairly recently published, which contained this passage: 'The whole subject (rare and genuine old primroses) is fraught with so many complications that the person who dares to write upon it with only some four or five years' experience behind him runs the gauntlet of endless comment and criticism.' That not very encouraging statement, insofar as it concerns double primroses, very accurately describes myself. It is only five years ago that I started to cultivate them seriously.

About four years before that date I saw in a cottage garden my first variety of all, the double white. Old gnarled plants they were, and rather resembled their owners. I was given two or three clumps which I tore to bits in the light-hearted manner in which anyone would divide a casual and unwanted polyanthus. I planted out the pieces in the tiny garden of a cottage I rented at the time in the Isle of Man. There was little cover or shade and the winds were heavily salt-laden. But the plants flourished as they always do near the sea, and one even set seeds—the only plant of the thousands that I have grown to do that naturally. Bear in mind that I knew nothing of the many double primrose theories and contradictions. To me, they were just very attractive flowers.

Double Primroses

A cow made a placid meal of most of my seedlings and only about a dozen were saved. The original plants and the seedlings were taken to my home outside Bristol where again they flourished, but the seedlings produced only ordinary primrose flowers and were discarded. 'The gauntlet of endless comment . . .' the obvious comment on my action is—'the man is a lunatic'. That would be fair enough if lunacy is that state of mind that makes one do things through ignorance, although maybe ignorance saved me from much later disappointment. A curious thing happened to one or two of the double white plants, and also to one or two that I had given away for, by the following spring they had become really enormous and then produced a very heavy crop of small ordinary single primroses. I know of no explanation for this, and it is quite certain that it had occurred to double white primrose plants and that there were no wild primroses mixed up with them. I have been asked frequently since then if double primroses revert. To the best of my knowledge they do not and certainly nothing like it has ever happened with any of my plants since. There is, however, a note in *Gardening Illustrated* for 1904, to the effect that the double lilac very occasionally reverts to single (Alex Dean confirms this elsewhere) but that this is the only variety that ever does so. That, however, does not explain the change I witnessed from double white to ordinary single wild primroses.

In the spring of 1948 I found two patches of Marie Crousse in my garden which must have been at least three years old and were growing in almost naturalized conditions. This variety is, to my mind, more attractive when grown in this way. It is neater and the flowers seem to be more in proportion compared with those on yearling plants. The patches were broken up and planted out in some newly broken ground beneath standard apple trees, where they grew well in spite of the ground becoming very wet in winter. It is difficult to give accurate figures but I would say that the original forty to fifty pieces have, in five years, provided up to five thousand plants. If this is hard to credit, it must be remembered that they have been deliberately split up to make as big a commercial stock as possible in as short a time as possible.

In the late autumn of 1948 my son and I acquired a small stock of double white and double lilac and planted them in the same area. We also heard of a plant of double sulphur. By now our interest and enthusiasm were thoroughly aroused. We asked in many cottages (never with success) for double primroses, and were often told, 'No, I haven't any but I remember my Granny used to grow them in her garden.' We were given this answer so often that it seemed obvious to us that the secret for growing them must lie in the age-old fertility of a cottage garden. To have appreciated this one simple point is the only merit that either of us is ever likely to claim, and we did our very best to interpret it.

To digress. One generous application of manure will only produce fertility for one year, or two at the most. But the cottage gardens received this every year, so that what remained from one year became mixed with the soil when the new application was dug in during the next. Over a period of time the whole ground to the depth of cultivation would have become thoroughly mixed with manure in various stages of decomposition. To achieve this, as market gardeners, we argued that the mechanical rotary cultivator that we use could do to our soil in a comparatively few minutes what it had taken very many years of manual cultivation to do in cottage gardens, provided we could find enough suitable manure. Our way out of this problem was to buy a considerable quantity of spent mushroom-bed compost and to put it on the beds thick—very thick. To it we added about one sixth of the amount in peat and then cultivated the bed to a depth of about nine inches. By this means we obtained a uniform mixture from the surface to the depth of cultivation. Since then, chiefly through the generosity of a farmer neighbour, we have tried other forms of organic manure. Rightly enough he changes the subject when asked for farmyard manure, but assumes an air of great benevolence when he has a large pile of wet chaff or debris from a bean stack which he cannot burn but would like removed. His benevolence takes the very kind and practical form of lending us a tractor and trailer and we now cart away as many tons of both as we can get. This, we find, produces as good results as the mushroom compost, particularly if it is mixed with the soil in not too rotted a condition.

Double Primroses

The year 1950 was in some ways critical. We were told that double primroses were 'hard to grow', 'impossible to grow', or 'might grow', and many other twists of the same sentiment. A foreman in a very big nursery told us that double primroses could only be grown if one had a stream in the garden with suitable banks, and that his nursery had spent a lot of money in buying stock only to lose the lot. Yet we had the evidence of our own eyes in contradiction for here our primroses were growing very well indeed. That autumn we went over to Malvern to see Mr. Ernest Ballard, who has since died, and his Michaelmas daisies, and we confided in him. What a grand enthusiast he was! I shall always keep a mental picture of him, with some garden tool in his hand, threatening us with fearful forms of physical violence if we took the slightest notice of anyone and failed to accept what our common sense told us. Certainly he did us a great deal of good and gave us a reasonable amount of confidence in ourselves.

In the spring of 1949 we had a most extraordinary experience. A friend came in and said that he had discovered a double primrose in an absolutely derelict garden that adjoined his. Except from what local people said, it would be quite impossible to tell that the piece of ground had ever been a garden, for it was now only turf. 'In the interests of security' (to use an old and familiar phrase) I must disclose no more details except to say that, in all, we have collected about fifteen distinct varieties from this small area. At first we believed in our own concocted theory that these plants were relics of some former collection, but we are now quite certain that this is not the case. Every plant has had all the appearances of being a seedling. The root system has been very small indeed; the plant has had three or four very small leaves, and only a couple of tiny flowers. As they were collected they were washed out and then planted under the apple trees, where they made such growth that in some cases we were able to split them in the following autumn. From our experience of them it is evident that they have tremendous vigour, for under cultivated conditions they make roots of nine and more inches and the plant itself increases fast. Furthermore, they are true primroses, for 'the flowers do stand every one severally upon slender long footstalks as the single kind doth'.

By June of 1951, the space under the apple trees was no longer nearly large enough for the number of plants that we were going to deal with, and it became necessary to use a part of the field where there is no shade at all. We have, therefore, to shade the young plants artificially. This we do by covering them with hessian stretched on wires. However, this would be a most unsightly practice in a private garden so here the answer can easily be provided by a bed on the north side of a shed, wall, shrubs or even taller-growing plants. This last alternative is simple indeed, but a moment's reflection on the conditions under which a wild primrose grows will show that it is effective. The wild primrose flowers in March and April and, in that month, there are no hedgerow plants that are of any height. By the time that the primroses have finished flowering their neighbours—cow parsley, grasses, campions and the rest—are well into their spring growth, so that when the primroses are out of bloom the remaining vegetation is well above them, providing thick shade. By October this has flowered, seeded and died down, and there are the primroses with one or two great leaves from the past season and tight clusters of new leaves. Employing this argument, we over-planted three beds of double primroses, white, lilac and Crousse, with *Linaria marocanno*, but were not sufficiently skilful to control the density of seeds. The result was a near approach to the appearance of duck weed on a pond. Other pressing matters intervened until we eventually had to tackle a miniature jungle, but the primrose plants were still there. I am sure that there is a great deal to be said for the intimate shade of neighbouring plants. It is just a question of planning a border with this idea in mind, not minding, necessarily, if primroses are in the front; for other plants, like those in the hedgerows, are of no height when the primroses are in bloom. Surely this is how cottage gardeners have managed it through the centuries.

In all this one dare not get away from the soil conditions which double primroses demand. But are they so different from what so many herbaceous plants want? Consider them. Delphiniums, Michaelmas daisies, pyrethrums, phloxes, erigeron, solidago and the rest—is there one that would not be magnificent in 'a deeply-stirred and moderately rich soil in which the roots can descend freely in search of moisture'?

To return to my own first introduction to double primroses. Those plants that I saw that day must have been at the very least three years old. By that time, as in many single varieties, a plant will have made such enormous rootstocks that the new, young tufts of leaves are left up in the air with the result that it is almost impossible for them to produce young roots. Possibly if they were top-dressed all might be well, but how much more satisfactory to split them up after two years before their vigour starts to dwindle, and before the character of their growth has become such as almost to prohibit their continued existence.

I have stated that forty or fifty plants of Marie Crousse increased to five thousand plants in five years. Most of the varieties that we have grown and of which we have some experience can be supposed to increase on the same scale, although not all make such big individual plants. But there are large and not so large varieties of most plants. For instance, I doubt if Mme. Pompadour would ever grow as robustly as double white, but I am prepared to state emphatically that Pompadour will come excellently and prolifically from a rootstock. However, as long as she remains at the mink-coat price level it would be both unnatural and ungallant to think of her as vulgarly robust.

It is in June that we split our plants. At this time, and after the flowering season is over, the new young roots push out from the collar of each tuft of leaves, their length depending very much on the season. At least they should be sufficiently long to be able to support the young plant and, therefore, to continue to grow on their own without the help of the previous year's roots, which will now be seen to be coming out of a hard rootstock almost as thick and long as one's little finger. This can be clearly seen in the illustration of double primroses in Curtis's *Botanical Magazine* for 1794 (volume vii). Each tuft of leaves is gently torn from the root-stock after the whole plant has been thoroughly washed out. The point of washing a plant is to make certain that one can see what one is doing, to ensure removal of slugs' eggs, and to make an opportunity for passing the plants through some form of deterrent to aphides. We shorten down all young roots to about two inches. This helps to promote a vigorous root system and certainly makes the young plants easier to handle. If one has many plants to divide, it is clear that the last to be lifted will have grown very considerable new roots. There is, therefore, an ever-growing pile of earth, chopped off roots, bits of leaves, weeds and rootstocks—unless the last are deliberately collected—at the site where we divide. A month or two after, we find this mound literally covered with nice little primrose-leaf rosettes. Now if some hundreds of plants have been divided in that manner it stands to reason that only those rootstocks at the top of the pile could possibly produce these rosettes, for everything else will be turning into compost. So it is that if a rootstock is planted in the manner of a 'flag' iris, with the top portion above the surface of the soil, there is every chance that it will send up new growth which can be removed from the rootstock, sometimes in the following autumn, but certainly in the following June. The finest plant that we have ever exhibited of the variety 'Red Paddy', a plant that was literally solid with flowers, was planted as a rootstock the previous June and, when ultimately divided up, gave us nine plants.

Mention has been made of the condition of growth of a plant by June and it would be worthwhile to trace the growth further than that and so answer a question often asked—'When can double primroses be moved?' The young plant newly put out in June takes a certain time to recover. The first thing that happens is that all the leaves wilt in a most alarming way and eventually die right down. While this is going on the roots remain more or less dormant and then slowly start to grow. In four or five weeks very small rosettes of new leaves appear, so small indeed that I wonder every year if they can possibly turn into decent plants. But by September all is well, and by the end of the month buds appear in most varieties. Some writers in the gardening magazines at the end of the nineteenth and beginning of the twentieth centuries say that these should be picked off or the plant will lose its virility. Maybe this is wise advice, particularly for those districts where the winter is normally mild. But we leave them on for the snow and the frost to do the necessary picking, although, be it noted, neither snow nor frost does the plants themselves the slightest harm.

The fact that buds appear leads one to assume that root growth adequate to their support has been achieved. This we find to be definitely the case when we lift the plants at the end of October to fulfil orders. By then the root system is assuming its final shape. This can be described as a half circle with some roots running along just below the surface of the soil and the remainder from there to the vertical. This is an important point and it seems to me to emphasize the need to obtain a thorough mixture of the original dressing of compost with the soil.

However, the crowns themselves have not increased. They remain as single crowns. The root system continues to grow in any period of open weather right on to the time of blooming. As a curious proof of this I record the fact that moles are our worst enemy. To increase the humus content of the soil is to create better and better conditions for worms, and they are a major part of a mole's diet. Furthermore the beds here are prepared just before the young plants are lined out in June, and by that time of the year the ground in general is becoming very hard. Thus the local moles suddenly find an area of very loose tilth containing food, and naturally they work in it. The reason why they always seem to work straight down a row of young plants is beyond my grasp but they certainly do. This has the effect of pushing the soil away from the young roots and consequently retarding their growth. Constant pressing down and the action of rain bring the soil back to them, with the result that many young plants which failed to get away at the beginning start to grow well in about November, and by spring they have become quite good plants. This is not the place to discuss ways and means of catching moles, and I will only say that the various methods that we have tried are not very successful.

As the flowering season approaches the crown thickens to some extent. If it is dug up and examined it will be seen that two or three immature crowns are forming round the main one, their stage of growth depending very much on the general rate of the whole plant since June. The main crown will give the major part of the crop of flowers, the secondary or latter part of the crop coming from the younger crowns. Then as the flowers fade, the whole plant seems to expand and, by June, achieves the stage at which it can be split up.

Our experience is, therefore, that double primrose plants may be moved at any time from the beginning of October to the main flowering season, provided the weather is open. But it must be stressed that the reason for this lies in the growth of the root system and not in the top of the plant. Possibly the most marked example among the better-known varieties is furnished by Our Pat. Being a late-flowering plant, its crown is liable to remain most unconvincing until a short time before its flowering season, at which moment it starts to make growth fast. This variety is often best left undivided provided its situation is agreeable to it, until early September, and by then it is possible to split it up into ten or fifteen pieces.

Although many of the old writers advocated autumn division, we do not do so because of the condition of our soil at that time of the year. Ours is a peculiar field, probably part of the site of the community at the time of the Domesday Book, and various springs appear which are liable to make parts of it very wet. To offset the effect of these springs we dig ditches to take off as much surplus water as possible, but the ground still remains very wet. Now double primroses are not bog plants, neither do they require, as the nursery foreman alleged, 'streams with suitable banks'. Like so many other plants they do not like water standing round their roots during the winter, although it is remarkable what they will tolerate. For example, when preparing to exhibit in 1951 we found water at the bottom of every hole made by digging up the plants that we required to take with us, yet the plants were robust. One cannot suppose that the water had been there throughout the winter because there had been heavy rain a few days previously, but the water table cannot have been much lower.

We have very little experience of insect pests and diseases. We believe, rightly or wrongly, that to create conditions in which a plant can grow strongly and healthily is to remove a good deal of the danger liable to be caused by disease. Each year our plants are moved on to fresh ground which, in the previous year, has grown crops whose general treatment has raised the fertility of the soil.

An obviously dangerous time occurs when the young plants are first lined out; as it is likely to coincide with hot weather, and they are, of course, at their weakest. Danger is, however, lessened by the thorough washing-out given to them. Red Spider is said to be a common enemy, but we have not experienced it, and we have been told in letters that slugs do great harm. Damage is more easily seen in the case of a few plants than it is with thousands which cannot be scrutinized so closely. Although slugs are common with us, we have not noticed them doing any particular damage to our primroses. In any case the various slug deterrents are very effective.

We have tried to make double primroses bloom earlier than usual by employing cloches. Last year a hundred or so plants were clochèd on the first of December but the effect was to draw up the leaves, to cause a number of the secondary buds to die, and to make the first flowers bloom only a week before plants that had been cloche-covered for three weeks. But cloches are extremely useful for two purposes—first, to keep a strip of ground in good condition in the winter if it is desired to split up plants later than is normal. The ground remains drier and warmer and the newly moved plants will grow to some extent. However, attention must be paid to ventilating the cloches in spells of really warm weather. In the second place, cloches are invaluable for presenting flowers in the best possible condition for some special purpose such as a show or other occasion. For example, this spring we had to provide a considerable quantity of double white primroses for a wedding, and the plants were clochèd up a fortnight before the date of picking.

Now I come to a difficult point, maybe a heresy, for I am touching upon people's general background knowledge. There is unquestionably a good deal of pessimistic and destructive thought and writing concerning these plants which are our subject. One reads such phrases as 'I remember when I was a child', or 'I remember my grandmother telling me that when she was a child', or, 'It is a very old variety', or, 'It has always been difficult to cultivate'. When one stops to consider some of these phrases they mean very little, and certainly give one no factual knowledge. It is easy to evade the issue behind vague sentences. But if that sort of thing is said often enough it is bound, in the end, to give a bad reputation.

Much can be learnt at shows. When we show we offer only double primroses with nothing else to distract the attention. Some people, elderly folk, suddenly see their nostalgic memories become fact again and their interest is a very real pleasure to see. Many have not the slightest idea what double primroses are. They have never heard of them but their interest is stimulated by the beauty of the plants themselves. Then there are the doubters, who once grew them but then they lost their plants. Is it too much to suggest that those who wish to grow these lovely plants, again or for the first time, should so arrange their orders that they have at least two plants of a variety instead of one plant only of each of several varieties? There is a danger in giving a single plant too much care. No one is likely to divide up a solitary plant in the same light-hearted manner as several, and the chances are that it will be left in the ground when it should have been split up. Then it will die and, being the only plant, that is the end except, probably, for another addition to a bad reputation. Finally, at shows, there are the few—mercifully only a few—who contemplate double primroses and then ask the world to witness the folly of nurserymen who cannot leave well alone and must even do awful things to 'the beautiful wild primrose'.

I have made no attempt in this chapter to give an impression of scientific knowledge or even of knowledge that would enable one to make a particularly skilful approach to the growing of double primroses. Neither my son nor myself has had any scientific training whatsoever, and neither of us has lifelong experience of the nursery trade. If a plant looks wrong to us for some reason that is not sufficiently obvious, we enlist the help of the County Horticultural Adviser—help that has always been given in a most generous way—and our other step is to isolate the plant or variety. Neither have we attempted to raise a new variety from seed, or to produce seed for distribution.

Double Primroses

Note. Major Taylor is able to do the division of his plants in June on account of the dampness of his land. Those whose land is of a sandy, dry nature will be advised to leave the plants untouched during June, except when a rainy period is encountered, as in June 1953.—Roy Genders.

CHAPTER IX

Double Primroses for Amateurs

(by Roy Genders)

I
t is just twenty years since I began to collect single and double primroses, and ever since they have always appeared to me the most fascinating of all flowers. From a small beginning of Primula Wanda and Double White (*Alba plena*) has emerged a specialized commercial collection covering more than an acre of ground, but my interest really commenced in the immediate post-World War I days (1919), when at five years old I went to live with my grandparents in Sussex and there spent all my days picking primroses in the Storrington hedgerows in April and mushrooms in sight of Chanctonbury Ring in September. Ever since those carefree days the love of primroses and mushrooms has remained with me, and I cannot remember any time when I was not growing the two of them. A famous horticulturist said to me only this year (1953), 'my own view is that the doubles dropped out during this twentieth century because they were more trouble than they were worth.'

In this mechanical age of ease, perhaps to have to divide and mulch one's plants, however lovely they may be, is asking rather too much of the gardener. But what about the staking and constant tying of such plants as the delphinium and helenium? And surely it is much easier to increase one's stock by simple division of the small crowns as compared with the rooting and layering of carnation shoots or even the propagating of violas and pansies from cuttings? Even the scabious must have additional lime to flower to perfection. After division, provided a damp period is chosen, the small primrose shoots will require no attention until

Double Primrose, Quaker's Bonnet (Two-Year Plant)

A Polyanthus Border in the grounds of the
Royal Horticultural Society, Wisley

(Photograph J. E. Downward)

they come into bloom; a viola or carnation cutting will need constant attention as to watering and ventilation of frames. The primrose is a perennial and may be given attention when one has the necessary time; the half hardy and even the hardy annual must be given attention as to sowing, watering and pricking out the seedlings as the season and state of the plant demand.

Double primroses should have a supply of humus and some nitrogen to bring out the best in them and this is their only requirement apart from periodical division of the roots and replanting. Surely this is not too much to ask in return for their early spring charm year after year. I really believe that it has been the policy of the nurseryman, and the advent of large-scale advertising in the press, that have brought about the almost total extinction of the double primrose. 'Small profits, quick returns' has for long been the motto not only of Mr. Woolworth but also of the large plant nurseryman, and 'quick returns' have meant the rapid increase of a plant. For this reason the pansy raised from seed has been advertised to a much larger degree than the named viola propagated from cuttings, and likewise the polyanthus which comes readily from seed has appealed far more to the nurseryman than the slowly propagating double primroses. Except for the specialist grower, double primroses have never been a commercial proposition in an era concerned with getting a large turnover in the shortest possible time. This, I feel, has brought about the almost complete lack of knowledge of the double primrose with the past generation of gardeners. The selling of plants by mail order has almost completely taken the place of sales by the local nurseryman with his love of all plants, no matter how slow they are to propagate. Talking to a nurseryman of the 'old school' several years ago, I asked him about the doubles and quaint primrose types which he used to grow in quite large numbers. He replied, 'They are rarely asked for now, and the increased cost of running my business, due to the new agricultural wages, the high cost of coke and increased rates, makes it necessary for me to grow only popular lines now, much to my disappointment.' His 'popular lines' were wallflowers and forget-me-nots, polyanthus and annuals of every description, and some of the new perennials which are readily increased by root division. Rather than there being any difficulty with the cultivation of most of the doubles, the uneventful life of these plants, with consequent lack of news during the first half of the twentieth century, accounts for a generation of gardeners who have come and gone without any knowledge that doubles ever existed. My father, who until his passing possessed one of the most beautiful gardens in the district, famed far and wide for its magnificent delphiniums and for its greenhouse begonias, knew nothing of double primroses. He had neither seen nor grown a single variety; they were, indeed, unknown to almost all gardeners during the first half of the century. Those enthusiasts who are now taking considerable interest in the plants must not be discouraged by talk of their being difficult to grow. Indeed several varieties, as with all plants, are more exacting as to soil and care, but most of them will thrive under the roughest conditions. At my primrose gardens on the east coast of Yorkshire, where the plants receive spray from the wild North Sea and the maximum of cold winds, the plants, and particularly the doubles, grow with the utmost vigour, just as they did in the equally exposed part of north Staffordshire where they also received a fair share of the soot and smoke deposits from the Potteries. Two of the most successful primrose nurseries are situated near Aberdeen, where the Bon Accords were raised in 1900; another is near Inverness. Here, often frozen into the ground for weeks on end, the plants bloom to perfection in late spring. Yet another commercial primrose grower is situated on the borders of barren Dartmoor where a summer sun beats down unmercifully from April to September. When I was visiting the nursery after a five weeks' freedom from rain (until three days before my visit, when it poured for a full twenty-four hours) I was told that the plants had been given no water and that they had appeared quite shrivelled. Three days after a thorough soaking the centres were growing out fresh green, and on my second visit a week later they looked in perfect condition. So much for their ability to withstand contrasts in climatic conditions. It may be said that they will grow to perfection along the north coast of Scotland, on the exposed east coast of Yorkshire, in the centre of

Devonshire and, as is so well known, throughout the whole length and breadth of Ireland. Could any plant be more accommodating? As far as climate is concerned, they are in no way eccentric.

Now as to soil. I have cultivated *Alba plena*, Marie Crousse, Bon Accord Gem, Our Pat, Red Paddy and Quaker's Bonnet under field conditions in a soil containing only the minimum amount of humus, provided in the form of well-decayed leaf mould. The plants were left entirely to their own resources and increased rapidly, besides covering themselves with a wealth of bloom. These six varieties, however, may be classed as decidedly easy growers, and should be those selected to begin a collection. They are possessed of tremendous vigour, will succeed almost anywhere, and will grow well in window boxes too.

Then come what may be termed the fairly easy varieties, those that will grow and bloom well only if given some assistance in the way of humus and nitrogen, for instance some horticultural peat or leaf mould to which is added a small quantity of animal manure, hop manure or wool shoddy. Many growers are also poultry keepers, and double primroses thrive on dried poultry droppings mixed with chopped straw or chaff. Spent hops, too, are generally to be obtained for the asking at any large brewery, or hop manure of a proprietary make may be bought at the local seed stores. A small quantity dug into the soil and augmented with some peat or leaf mould will be all that is necessary to grow these rather more difficult doubles to perfection. Seaweed, too, for those who live near the sea, is most useful. Farmyard manure, where it can be obtained, will provide both humus and nitrogen. Wool shoddy, cheap to buy and so easy to handle, will also supply both humus and nitrogen. Each of these materials is cheap and easy to use and they are only the same substances that are necessary to grow a quality crop of cauliflowers or brussels sprouts, the supplying of which the gardener takes as a matter of course. The doubles which come into this category are Curiosity; most of the Bon Accords with the exception of Lavender and Gem which are easy, Crimson King; Chevithorne Purple, which in some soils is very easy; Delmonden Mauve, French Grey and Double Cream.

99

In the 'difficult' class seems to be the old Madame Pompadour, Arthur Du Moulin and all the yellows, and each year they become more difficult to find. It may be that some growers have at one time purchased plants of one of the yellow doubles only to have their enthusiasm damped by failure. This is anything but a fair test, but may have branded all the doubles as 'difficult'. Plants in this section may be nursed to perfection by providing a partially shaded position, by supplying them with humus, and by attending to their moisture requirements in a dry period. One thing they do demand, and that is frequent lifting and division of the roots and the removing of old rootstock. As has been mentioned already, the doubles tend to push themselves out of the soil, always forming fresh roots above the level of the soil. I make no apologies for repeating that either the plants must be given a yearly mulch or have fresh soil drawn up to the stem, or they must be lifted and re-planted with the new roots beneath soil level. Double primroses are still one of the most labour-saving plants of the garden. They require no staking and no disbudding, no cutting down of rank and dead foliage, no tidying of the shoots as for carnations, and they never cause trouble by overhanging paths and lawns.

Where possible, the doubles should be planted not later than early November so that they become well established before winter. If they are moved just before they bloom, flowering will be delayed; and if moved when in bloom, the flowers die away. In this they differ from the singles and hose-in-hose. To those who are to form a collection of doubles, may I suggest purchasing the plants in autumn so that they may flower undisturbed in all their glory the following spring.

Excessive winter moisture should be guarded against as far as the doubles are concerned. Like pinks they will withstand any amount of cold and frost, but in too much moisture they do not thrive. A heavy clay soil may be made more 'open' by incorporating the necessary humus and a quantity of grit (ashes) or coarse sand. Plants growing in an excessively light soil will require a mulch every June.

Those wishing to exhibit their plants, and the Northern Section of the National Auricula and Primula Society hold their Annual

Show in Manchester on the first Saturday of each May (the Midland Section, the previous week), should commence with these robust varieties that are successful as pot plants. There are sections to cover every class of primrose, even a special class for novices. Those doubles which bloom well as a pot plant, and they should be lifted into the pots very early in spring, are Tyrian Purple, Marie Crousse, Red Paddy, Burgundy, Bon Accord Gem, Bon Accord Purity and the old Double White.

Rather than make a selection of twenty different varieties, one would have far more satisfying results by growing two plants of each of ten varieties. With all plants it is possible that one may die off here and there and the double primrose is no exception. However, where this does occur, that particular variety, even though it may be the robust Marie Crousse, is branded as being 'difficult', which is most unfair. During the cold spring of 1953 it was my misfortune to lose a number of sweet pea plants but it would be ridiculous to call the sweet pea a plant incapable of surviving the spring climate of the north.

The double primrose will always be a connoisseur's plant, from the easy Quaker's Bonnet which may be purchased for 2s. 6d. to the now rare and slow-to-increase Bon Accord Elegance, priced at two guineas or more. The reason is that they cannot be grown from seed like calendulas or pansies, and only a few specialist growers are prepared to spend their time and energies on the commercial cultivation of these choice and fascinating plants. In any case there would be no fun in finding a pearl in every oyster; but it is worth trying.

CHAPTER X

Named Varieties of Double Primroses

The authors believe this to be the very first attempt to produce a classified list of the named varieties of double and single primroses. References have been found in which writers affirm that one should be made, but we have not succeeded in finding any. We are only too well aware of the inadequacy of this attempt but we hope that it will at least provide some foundation for the future, as ninety varieties of doubles are listed.

Against each variety is shown the earliest date known to us, its reference, and anything that appears of interest, whether of general interest or only concerning the cultivation. Inevitably many people may quarrel with the descriptions, but the quotations show how the varieties appeared to those who wrote about them at the time. It will be noticed how few varieties have ever been given any award by the Royal Horticultural Society, presumably because few have been put forward. So we are unfortunately denied this authoritative source.

As there seems to be a great deal of confusion about the sulphurs, yellows and primrose-coloured varieties, these are dealt with in a separate section.

So far as possible it has been decided to keep to the original descriptions, provided that they are sufficiently full. Correspondence from various private growers and nurserymen indicates that they can remember certain details of a variety which was common thirty years ago but, with deference, we beg to leave to doubt that memory can be as accurate as that unless detailed records were made at the time and are still available now. If that should be the case, then it would certainly be an excellent thing. But failing that we persist in thinking that the earliest-known full description should be the accepted one.

Early catalogues have also been consulted. Unhappily there are many gaps in the collection in the Lindley Library and none of the early established nurserymen is fully represented. It is a debatable point whether catalogue descriptions are really accurate, but in the absence of other and better particulars they have been used. In each case the nurseryman's name is inserted in brackets but is easily distinguishable from reference to gardening periodicals in any case.

ALBA PLENA. Easy to grow but now becoming scarce. Mentioned and illustrated by Gerard in his *Historie of Plantes* (1597). A lovely double, very free flowering and of the purest white.

ARMARANTHINA PLENA. This is an old variety about which little is known. The bloom is a very deep shade of crimson-red. This may be Madame Pompadour, as it is very similar in colour, or even Brilliant. A point worthy of attention is the slight variations in colours of all primroses in different parts of the country; this circumstance may have given rise to the carrying of different names by varieties which may be plants of the same origin. The same colour variation appears to a more marked degree with chrysanthemums.

ARTHUR DE SMIT. During the latter part of the nineteenth century this lovely variety was to be found in English gardens though it now seems to be extinct. It was raised either in Germany or Belgium and was a lovely shade of deep purple, edged buttercup-yellow. Would that it could be obtained to-day!

ARTHUR DU MOULIN. 1884. *The Garden*. '. . . one of the way of platypetala but called Dumillon'. It is not possible to say whether this wording meant that there was a similarity between the two varieties or whether, in fact, they were the same. Various spellings of the name occur—Dr. Arthur Dumoulin (*Gardening World*, 1885), Arthur Dumollin (*The Garden*, 1891), and so on, but we have found no evidence, either directly or by inference in the spelling, that this variety was named after the Irish family of De Molyns, the family name of Lord Vertry, though it may be so.

This variety has been widely used as a pollen parent in attempting to raise new varieties of double primroses.

(*The Garden*, 1891, Richard Dean). '. . . pale purplish lilac, very free, producing flowers on polyanthus stems.' It comes in bloom very early, possibly the first of the doubles.

BON ACCORDS

Probably 1904. This whole group was raised by the brothers Cocker of the famous Aberdeen nursery, who worked on these doubles at the suggestion of Mr. Murray Thomson, then living in Angus. In their catalogue for 1904, they offered 'seedlings from a fine strain available' but gave no further explanation.

They are described as polyanthus-primroses or bunch primroses, that is plants some of whose flowers are true primroses, while others appear on a polyanthus stem, both types coming from the same plant.

BEAUTY. A dark purple-blue flower with a very thin white margin to the petals. Some appear to be speckled white on the edges.

BLUE. Large flowers of deep blue. Markedly polyanthus. Very scarce and an outstanding variety.

BRIGHTNESS. Bright purplish-crimson. (*Gardening Illustrated*, 1935). Now seems extinct.

CERISE. Slightly deeper and a brighter rose than Gem. More dwarf in habit and scented. A strong grower but becoming rare.

CREAMY WHITE. As its name implies.

CRIMSON. Dark crimson. (*Gardening Illustrated*, 1935).

ELEGANS. Considered the finest of the Bon Accords. Rosy pink flower profusely flecked with white. F.C.C. Very difficult to grow.

GEM. Rose-coloured, tinted with lilac. A strong grower.

JEWEL. A very deep purple, reverse of petals flushed crimson.

LAVENDER. Light rosy-mauve, polyanthus stem, free-flowering and vigorous.

LILAC. A light shade of rosy-lilac, very free-flowering and easy. F.C.C.

Named Varieties of Double Primroses

PRIMROSE. Pale sulphur. Originally called Bon Accord Yellow but now extinct. (*Gardening Illustrated*, 1935).

PURITY. The only pure white in this group although its flowers are tinged with cream. The flowers form a more compact rosette than those of the old double white primrose. The base of the petals is slightly tinged with green.

PURPLE. Large purple flowers with a definite shade of blue on the reverse side of the petal. Markedly polyanthus.

ROSE. (*Gardening Illustrated*, 1935). Appears to be quite extinct.

SALMON. (*Gardening Illustrated*, 1935). Both the last two varieties are included in a very long list of double primroses in the paper mentioned, but this is the only reference that we have seen.

It is impossible to say whether this is a complete list of the varieties that were made available to the public, but the following letter, written by Mr. J. J. Stormont, to *Gardening Illustrated*, is of interest:

'It would be an impossible task to clear up the naming of Bon Accords. Messrs. Cocker raised a very large number of double varieties, of which many would never be named. They were not worth it. Then of some they never had sufficient stock to warrant naming. I bought a lot of these from the family after the nursery was given up.'

BRILLIANT. 1891. (*The Garden*). Richard Dean writes: 'Brilliant, a deep shining amaranth which I take to be the variety *Amarintha plena* which is much grown on the Continent and is apparently a rich-coloured form of the old double purple.'

BURGUNDY. 1914. (*Perry*). 'Synonym: *Sanguinea plena*. Rich crimson-purple.'

The expression '*Sanguinea plena*' is now applied to the variety Red Paddy which has nothing to do with Burgundy.

We believe, however, that the word 'burgundy' was originally used to describe the colour only, and not as a proper name, and that, therefore, the double primrose is ruby red. In recent catalogues it is also described as flecked with white.

BUXTON'S BLUE. 1901, but first shown at a Royal Horticultural Show in 1935, to be named 'Mrs. E. C. Buxton'; later given its present name. We quote from a letter very recently written to us by Mr. E. Hugh Buxton:

'The history of it is this. A great-uncle of mine, who lived at Bettws-y-Coed, was planting out a bed of single light-blue primroses. He had a few plants over and told his wife to throw them away. Instead she planted them in the kitchen garden and next year, walking round together, they found one was a double which flourished. When he died she sent me a plant of it as his nearest relation and young friend, and when she died it was named after her. It is a pure turquoise blue.'

CARNEA PLENA. The bluish-pink tinge on the outer petals provides the only difference between *Carnea* and *Alba Plena*.

CASTLEDERG. 1926. We are indebted to Mr. William Chalmers, the well-known nurseryman of Stonehaven, Kincardineshire, for our information on this variety. 'This was raised by a Mrs. Scott of Castlederg, Co. Tyrone. It was a chance seedling from some seed of her own saving and I was the first to obtain a plant of it.'

The flowers are very large and in colour a mixture of sulphur splashed with pink. The buds have a tendency to refuse to open in some seasons.

CHEVITHORNE PURPLE. Date unknown but probably the 1930s. We have been told that this variety was found in a garden in the West Country and have seen a plant that originally came from there. It is a double polyanthus with large flowers and the head so big that the stalk was not strong enough to keep it erect. The flowers a dark metallic purple-blue shade with the petals beautifully laced with white. A superb primrose and very easy to grow. There is also a pink form of similar habit.

CLARET. A variety widely grown during the late nineteenth century but now only in a few gardens. The bloom is the colour of Primula Wanda.

CLOTH OF GOLD. See under YELLOW-COLOURED.

CRIMSON KING. 1897. (T. Smith of Newry). 'Bright rosy crimson'. This description could not be applied to the variety sold to-day under this name. The present Crimson King is a bunch primrose with large purple-crimson flowers. In the correspondence in *Gardening Illustrated* of 1935 many writers state that it is 'the old Scotch red' or 'Scotch amaranthe'. It is certainly a very showy variety and is a reasonably strong grower.

CRIMSON EMPEROR. This is believed to be the variety sold to-day as Crimson King.

CRIMSON PADDY. 1935. (*Gardening Illustrated*). Moore includes this name in his list, but under the heading of varieties that he did not possess, and states that it is a crimson primrose with a wire edge of white. This is the only reference that we have seen to this name.

CURIOSITY. 1899. (Perry). 'Double polyanthus-primrose, yellow ground with scarlet, rose and bronze.' Further remarks relating to this variety are included under Golden Pheasant.

DELMONDEN MAUVE. 1939, raised by the late Dr. Amsler. In a letter that Dr. Amsler wrote to us in April 1952, he said of this variety, 'I raised it in 1939 by using the pollen of Mme. Pompadour on a dark-coloured primrose (*acaulis* type). I got three dozen seedlings; most were of a nasty colour and I threw them away. Delmonden Mauve was the only double primrose. The first flowers often appear single on one stem and may be singles, but when the "bunch" appears later it is double. It is very vigorous and I must have raised hundreds from that first root.'

DERNCLEUGHI. 1899. (Perry). 'Deep crimson heavily margined with gold.' This is a double polyanthus whose other name is Tortoiseshell. Both Stormont and Cocker put the second name in brackets after the variety in their catalogues. In the correspondence in *Gardening Illustrated* the 'deep crimson' is changed to 'dark brown' in two places, but in five different catalogues at the beginning of the century all describe it in similar words to Perry's.

DOUBLE CREAM. This is a lovely variety. The plants in Mr. Roy Genders's possession originally came from Co. Derry. The colour is a true Jersey-cream shade; the bloom is of excellent form. Quite easy to grow, given plenty of humus in the soil and regular division.

DOUBLE GREEN (a). This is not really a true double for it is caused by the sepals of the flower being developed as foliage leaves, a condition known as 'phyllody'. It is to be found occasionally among a batch of primroses in any part of the British Isles, but seems to be more prevalent in Ireland. For some unknown reason it is often called the 'Exeter' primrose. In appearance it is unique and interesting rather than beautiful.

DOUBLE GREEN (b). There is also a true double green, as mentioned by Parkinson, which was thought to be extinct; it is believed to have recently been re-discovered in a Dorset garden.

DOWNSHILL GROUP

1900 onwards. This whole group was raised by the late Mr. Murray Thomson. In 1905 he wrote to Professor Henslow, 'In the first generation I did not get one plant bearing double flowers, although I had used pollen from them. Saving seed from these single seedlings without any artificial fertilization I was surprised to find a good percentage of doubles, some of them very fine indeed; but what pleased me more was the great vigour with which they grew.' By 1911 some of his plants were becoming known, for in a report of a show in Edinburgh that appeared in *Gardening Illustrated* for 1911, we read:'. . . the advent of the new varieties, some of which were raised by Mr. P. Murray Thomson, will be welcome.'

It is interesting to note that the Rev. W. Murdoch confirms that Murray Thomson was responsible for suggesting to Cocker that the latter should try to raise new varieties from seed.

In Stormont's catalogue for 1930 double primrose seed is offered. 'We are pleased at last to be able to offer seeds to produce doubles. The seed has been grown by a gentleman who, working on Mendelian lines, has himself raised many fine doubles. No guarantee can be given that doubles will emerge but the raiser expects that a small percentage ought to be semi or full doubles.'

The next item in the catalogue is: '*P. Juliae* Hybrids from the same grower. The seed is from plants crossed to produce doubles.'

It is believed that the gentleman referred to was Mr. Murray Thomson, who resided in Hereford before moving to Scotland, and at least one variety mentioned in this chapter was raised from these seeds. It is likely that others were never named or generally released.

BLUEBIRD. 1930 A.M. 'foliage large, flowers double, 1⅜ inches in diameter, lavender-violet, very free-flowering.'

CAMBRIDGE BLUE. 1930 A.M. 'medium vigour, foliage large, flowers double, 1¼ inches in diameter, lavender blue.'

ENSIGN. Large bright-purple flowers borne on a long poly-anthus stem with short pedicels. A late-flowering variety which does best in shade. Appears to have *Juliae* blood in it.

BLUE COAT. No description available.

BLUE GOWN. Amethyst blue.

BLUE PETER. Amethyst blue.

BLUE ROBE. Amethyst blue. This and the last two varieties are mentioned by Moore in the correspondence in *Gardening Illustrated* in 1935, and he adds that none of the three was then in commerce, and we have found no further references to them.

PETUNIA. No description available.

PLUM. 1930 A.M. 'foliage large, flowers double, 1⅜ inches in diameter, mauve, very free flowering.'

PURPLE EMPEROR. 1936. (Stormont). 'rich deep purple-blue'.

VANITY. Described by Miss Hume as a *Juliae* hybrid, but no description is given.

Mention is also made in the *Gardening Illustrated* correspondence of St. Keverne, Blue Beard and Blue Velvet, but no descriptions are given of these either.

A characteristic of the Downshill Group is their smooth foliage.

FLAKE. See PRINCE SILVERWINGS.

FRENCH GREY. 1873. (Ware). 'double french white'. 1900 (Perry) 'creamy white'. The blooms appear to be a dirty white, the variety sometimes called DINGY.

GOLDEN BALL. 1898. (*The Garden*). 'A strong variety with large foliage and pink and yellow double flowers.' This variety and its description are dealt with in an article on double polyanthus. Golden Ball is mentioned as still being in cultivation in 1935, but it now seems extinct.

GOLDEN PHEASANT. 1898. (*The Garden*). The description of this variety is part of the same article as is mentioned in the previous paragraph. 'It is difficult to find a more beautiful flower than

Golden Pheasant with its wealth of rich golden-brown, perfectly double blossoms of which you may see six to ten on each stem.'

In 1912 McWatt gives this variety as a synonym for Curiosity, describing it as yellow and red; and the same confusion of names recurs in 1935 and again in 1946.

HARLEQUIN. 1888. (*The Garden*). 'Strong grower, lilac'. But in 1891 *The Gardener's Magazine* gives a more detailed description: 'rose, pencilled with white, a pale and mottled form of platypetala.'

At the beginning of this century there are various descriptions of Harlequin which state that it is red or crimson with a yellow centre, with the petals tipped with white. Most references state that it is a polyanthus.

JACQUES LIENHART. 1888. (*The Garden*). 'A great improvement on Marie Crousse, as it blooms later, and produces an abundance of darker-coloured flowers.' This is the only reference to this variety and from this description it doesn't appear to be better than Crousse.

KING THEODORE. 1884. (*The Garden*). 'Among polyanthus King Theodore, with blackish-crimson flowers, is very fine.' This is presumably the same variety as Rex Theodore.

MADAME POMPADOUR. See POMPADOUR.

MARIE CROUSSE. 1882. Royal Horticultural Society, *Journal*, March, A.M., but no description is given. In *The Garden* for 1882 there is, however, the following: 'blossoms one inch across and perfectly double, the petals forming a compact rosette of a rich lilac-purple.'

The Garden, 1884. 'The colour, a rich plum-purple, and an abundant flower.'

In an article in *The Gardener's Magazine* for 1901. we read: 'There is a good deal of confusion among them (double primroses) as, for instance, Marie Crousse or Croussiflora, as it is sometimes termed, can be found in three or four different forms, which is unfortunate and confusing.'

Helen Champernowne writes in *The Garden* of 1902. 'I send also a bloom of the real Marie Crousse, a double primrose as identified by Mr. R. Dean, Messrs. Barr and Sons and others. Why is it that a totally different Marie Crousse is now recognized as true Marie

Crousse? I send you this also. The old is a very late blooming variety; my specimen is hardly out, and it is most rare. You will notice that it is of a reddish crimson, spotted with white. The modern variety is pinkish lilac, and as Marie Crousse is often spoken of as Crousse's lilac, it seems to me that the old variety might be re-named with advantage, or that they should be called Red Marie Crousse and Lilac Marie Crousse. The lilac variety is a fairly early bloomer and the habit is different.'

The editor's description of the flowers sent by Helen Champernowne is:

'Marie Crousse (true)—large flowers of a pleasant low-toned rosy colour.

'Lilac Marie Crousse—a good flower of bright lilac colour.'

1891. (Ware). 'fine bold habit, flowers abundant, polyanthus heads of a rich colour, edged white.'

We include this reference as it is the only one that we have seen up to 1912 that makes any mention of a white edging. Nevertheless, the present-day variety would not normally be called polyanthus. Its description is as follows: the flowers of a reddish mauve, lavishly and irregularly marked with white, are large and are borne on long pedicels from a very short polyanthus stem. Some flowers are true primroses. A strong grower, but not as free flowering as some varieties.

MONT BLANC. 1881. (Carter). 'pure white'.

NEGRO. 1891. (*The Garden*). 'blackish maroon, very showy and fine'. This is doubtless the same variety as *Nigra plena*, which is described in 1897 as 'one of the darkest double primroses we have seen, the flowers very deep and richly coloured'; and by Stormont in 1911 as 'deepest purple, very dark'.

OLD IRISH RED. Originating in Co. Tyrone and a lovely deep red of true primrose habit. It flowers profusely and propagates easily.

ORIGINAL. 1891. (*The Garden*). 'clear purplish lilac—large and double, each petal having a margin of white.'

OUR PAT. 1935. (T. Smith of Newry). 'In a batch of *P. Juliae* one plant with distinct and purple-tinted vigorous foliage was noted, and when it flowered turned out to be a double purple with sapphire sheen, in certain lights a shade of blue. It was named

Pat after my youngest daughter. When a lady wrote challenging my right to use the name, as she had already raised a *Juliae* seedling which she had christened Pat, I replied that she could stick to that and I would call our plant "Our Pat".'

This is a bunch primrose, and very prolific and vigorous.

PADDY. 1897. (T. Smith of Newry). The entry in Smith's catalogue reads as follows: 'Crimson Purple (Paddy).' Occasionally one meets with references to Irish Paddy which must, we think, indicate this variety, the word 'Irish' being added to the name because of the location of Smith's nursery. In 1898 Forbes describes it as 'bright red', which is a very different thing, and his variety may have been, for a similar reason, Scotch Paddy.

PEARL. 1880. (Clibran). 'white'.

PLATYPETALA. 1871. (Lievin de Cock, a Belgian nurseryman). But he gives no description.

1879. Royal Botanical Society. 'A Botanical Certificate awarded to primrose *Platypetala flore plena*, exhibited by Paul and Son. A charming double primrose with flowers of a deep rich purple.' This is borne out in *The Garden* of 1882 which states: 'The peculiarly bright purple colour of the compact rosettes is very showy.' But later we find in *The Garden* of 1891, 'other varieties are *Platypetala plena* (A. Dumoulin), pale purplish-lilac, a good grower and very free, but which produces its flowers on polyanth stems; the grower gets a good head of bloom on this variety, but the flowers lack shape and size.' In the same year *The Gardener's Magazine* description is 'pale purple, very free, but giving small and ill-formed flowers on polyanth stems'.

There is a clear difference between the first two definitions and any that follow. In recent accounts the term 'platypetala' has invariably been given as a synonym for Arthur Dumoulins, but we think that the evidence shows that they are, in fact, two different varieties, the older one probably now being extinct.

POMPADOUR. 1879. (*The Gardener's Chronicle*). Richard Dean writes, 'An assumed variety, known as Mme. de Pompadour, does not appear to differ from the ordinary double crimson.' In *The Garden* of 1888 there is a very attractive coloured plate entitled 'Pompadour or Double Crimson'.

Polyanthus, Munstead Strain

Double Primroses from a print of 1793
(Note formation of new roots above old rootstock)

No recent account of this variety gives us much information about its cultivation, but an early account is more explicit: 'What a lovely one is this! It is getting very scarce; but if it be constantly divided, supplied with liberal top-dressings of well rotted manure and leaf-mould mixed, all through the summer, and well watered, it will increase rapidly.'

PRINCE SILVERWINGS. 1897. (T. Smith of Newry). 'The flowers come in various stages of doubling, and are a pretty combination of lilac-crimson with silver edging.'

1898. (*The Garden*). The Rev. P. H. Mules writes, 'The charming semi-double flake or, as it is known in Ireland, Prince Silverwings, a silver-laced polyanthus of great merit of which a proportion of the blooms are single, others duplex, others again quite double.' In the 1902 volume of this paper the description of this variety is augmented by the addition of 'strong orange blotches at the base of the petals'.

Prince Silverwings is one of the few double primroses that yield pollen and is, in consequence, often used for raising seed. Its value is therefore considerable.

QUAKER'S BONNET, LADIES' FAVOURITE, LILAC QUEEN AND LADIES' DELIGHT. These are locally popular names for the double lilac primrose (*Lilacina plena*) but we have found no reference to show that any of them have ever been universally used; though possibly Quaker's Bonnet is more common to-day. This is a charming variety, very easy to grow. The foliage is a deep sage green, the bloom being prolific and of a delightful pure pale mauve. Believed to be the double form of PRIMULA ALTIACA. (Sibthorpii).

CUMBERLAND QUEEN. Believed to be a new variety but no details known.

IRISH MOLLY. A lovely variety with blooms of a unique cherry red, similar in colour to the new *Juliae* single Tiny Tim.

LADY ISOBEL. A new yellow said to carry a bloom of deep gold, but this variety has not yet been seen by the authors.

LANARTH. Introduced in 1935, but no details can be given.

MARGOT. A new primrose having bloom of a delicate salmon colour, but this may be Salmonae, an old variety now believed almost extinct. This latter variety has also been called Bon Accord Salmon, but no such variety ever existed.

PAULINE HAWKES. Raised in Cheshire in 1949, by Capt. C. Hawkes. It is a strong grower and the bloom is a brilliant shade of terra-cotta, a much-needed colour in this group.

ROSEA PLENA. A very old variety, now almost extinct, but what a beauty! The colour is of pure coral pink, the petals being of star-shaped formation.

ROSE DU BARRI. A very rare variety, said to have been raised in France, where the lovely rose-pink bloom was seen by the authors. This variety was recently discovered again in an Irish garden and re-named Wingfield, though it may be a new variety altogether.

ST. AVAILA GLORY. A new variety but no description can be found.

QUEEN VICTORIA. 1893. (*The Garden*). 'Royal Horticultural Society, A.M. Polyanthus. A vigorous grower with large laced flowers which are disposed to be semi-double—shown by Cocker. Said to be an old variety re-introduced.' We believe this to be a double black polyanthus but have no definite information about the colour of the lacing.

RED PADDY. 1935. (*Gardening Illustrated*). 'Bright rosy crimson with white edge.' Another writer in the same correspondence states: 'Red Paddy is not *Amarantha plena*; it is a different variety. The real Red Paddy is a polyanthus type, with a thin wire edge of white. I have no doubt about the white edge on Red Paddy.' We would add that the flowers are noticeably flatter than those of other varieties. It is early flowering and sweet-scented. It also passes under the name of *Sanguinea plena*.

REGINA. 1900. (*The Garden*). Helen Champernowne sent a flower of this variety which the editor described as 'a fine flower of a magenta-crimson colour'. Now appears extinct.

REX THEODORE. 1899. (Barr). 'Double black polyanthus'. In the same year Perry gives it a similar description. But in *The Garden* of the preceding year it is described as 'a combination of rich crimson and yellow with each petal deeply fringed pure white'.

Named Varieties of Double Primroses

SCOTCH RED. 1874. (*Florist and Pomologist*). 'Forms a section by itself, being quite distinct ... blooms very early and freely ... foliage large, rounded and vigorous, and of a deep green hue, rather rough and uneven. Flowers are purplish-red in colour, not so full, and having an orange-buff base to the centre petals. Occasionally it throws up a short polyanthus stem.

1876. (*Gardener's Magazine*). 'One of the least double, a pale purplish red.' One correspondent in *Gardening Illustrated* in 1935 suggests that this variety is the same as Crimson King, but from our experience of the latter, this could not be so. Could it be Crimson Emperor?

TARTARICA. 1882. (*The Garden*). 'This plant was commonly grown a few years ago round Dublin. Known as *Primula tartarica*, the flower is described as being very double, of medium size, and in colour a lightish brown, nearly coffee-coloured, with a distinctly pencilled edge of golden yellow. Flowers each upon a single stem were borne well above the foliage which was not, in any particular, distinguishable from that of the common double lilac or white of our gardens.'

TORTOISESHELL. See DERNCLEUGHI.

TYRIAN PURPLE. 1935. (*Gardening Illustrated*). 'One of the newer hybrids.' We have also seen it described as 'the old Cornish primrose' in contemporary catalogues, but have found no reference to this elsewhere. A superb variety, having bloom the size of a two-shilling piece, and of a vivid bluish-mauve colour. Very easy.

WILSON (MRS. A. M.). 1930. A brick-red double polyanthus raised by Rev. Murdoch from a packet of seed obtained from Stormont and produced by Murray Thomson. By all who have grown or seen it, said to be outstanding in every way.

YELLOWS OR SULPHURS

There is the greatest confusion concerning the Sulphurs, which we may well make worse in our attempts to unravel. It must be borne in mind, from the outset, that double primroses can be found growing wild among their single brethren and we know that this has been so since the days of Parkinson. It is, therefore, reasonable to assume that all the varieties that were given names at the end of the nineteenth century were chance discoveries, and were only perpetuated because of the enthusiasm of those who found them or because they were good enough to attract the notice of a nurseryman who, therefore, propagated and distributed them. Therefore, in attempting to verify the existence, or otherwise of the early named varieties, contemporary references must be of particular value.

As an example of what may be found we mention a variety that we possess and which we rank as one of the best of all the varieties, of all colours. It was found in a wood in Devonshire. Its flowers are perfectly symmetrical rosettes and considerably larger than those of the double white primrose. They are carried on long stalks above good strong foliage. In every way it has all the appearance of a highly cultivated plant and not that of a chance wilding.

Finally, we feel that the use of the various colour terms such as yellow, sulphur, primrose, brimstone, straw and so on, must be made with reserve. There is, doubtless, a technical difference between them, but very little is made in colloquial speech.

EARLY SULPHUR. 1874. (*Florist and Pomologist*). 'Earliest to bloom, foliage long, narrow, rather glossy, smooth and somewhat relaxed. Flowers pale sulphur colour and borne very freely' . . . 'distinct' (1875, *Gardener's Magazine*) . . . 'remarkably early' (1876, *Gardener's Magazine*).

LATE YELLOW. 1874. (*Florist amd Pomologist*). 'Robust grower, dark green foliage, rough and uneven. Flowers extra large and distinct orange buff base to each petal, stout rounded form of flower buds.'

GIANT YELLOW. 1874. (*Florist and Pomologist*). 'Flowers of same size as Late Yellow but a shade lighter, foliage narrow and pointed, moderate growth . . . large, grand petals with a kind of double corolla of short petals in the centre' (1874, *Villa Gardener*) . . . 'bright yellow, large and fine' (1875, *Gardener's Magazine*) . . . 'more pointed buds and smoother foliage than Late Yellow' (1876, *Gardener's Magazine*).

GIANTESS YELLOW. 1874. (*Florist and Pomologist*). 'Richest

yellow hue, close resemblance to Giant Yellow, late bloomer . . .
very like the large sulphur' (1874, *Villa Gardener*) . . . 'the deepest
yellow' (1876, *Gardener's Magazine*) . . . 'I send you flowers, buds
and leaves of one that I have long known as Giantess. As you will
see, this has very short blunt buds, hairy stems, smallish leaves,
densely hairy' (1889, *The Garden*).

CLOTH OF GOLD (1). 1880. (*Gardener's Magazine*). 'Double
Primrose, Cloth of Gold, of which, Messrs. James Carter have the
stock, is the finest thing of its class we have yet seen. The flowers
are perfect rosettes with no tendency to duplication by which
many sorts of double primroses lose their symmetry of form . . .
the petals being in perfect order, with only one centre to each
flower. The colour is delicate primrose yellow. Some of the
flowers measure nearly two inches over the face' . . . The Royal
Horticultural Society Floral Committee awarded the F.C.C. to
Cloth of Gold which was described as 'a beautiful sulphur yellow
primrose with perfectly double flowers . . . so double, indeed, as
to form pretty compact rosettes. It is, moreover, a big grower
and profuse bloomer' (1881, *The Garden*).

But *The Gardener's Chronicle* for 1880 writes: 'Cloth of Gold
double primrose. I send you, for comparison, flowers and leaves
of this new double yellow primrose and the same of the old Late
Double Yellow variety. The former was obtained from Messrs.
Carter and Co., the latter from plants obtained from Scotland and
elsewhere. I have no doubt that Carter and Co., and the Floral
Committee shared the same opinion when it was awarded a F.C.C.
that it was a new and distinct variety. I doubted its distinctness at
the time.' (Editor's Note: 'We can see little or no difference
between them.')

We suggest that the definitions of the variety Cloth of Gold that
follow show that there were, in fact, two distinct varieties under
the one name, and we here distinguish them by the numerals (1)
and (2). It is established that Messrs. Carter possessed the stock of
what was obviously a magnificent plant, and it seems certain that
theirs would have been colloquially known as 'Carter's' to distinguish one from the other.

CLOTH OF GOLD (2). 1885. (*Journal of Horticulture*). 'A rich lemon yellow, very double and rather late, quite distinct from the rest ... I need scarcely state that the late Giant Yellow and Cloth of Gold are one and the same' (1885, *Gardening World*) ... 'long-shaped buds, large bright green foliage' (1889, *The Garden*) ... 'Cloth of Gold, very like to the Giant Yellow' (1890, *The Garden*).

Capt. Hawkes says of this variety, 'It has a habit of growing very well for a few years and then disappearing.'

In the correspondence in *Gardening Illustrated* of 1935, mention is made several times of 'Carter's Cloth of Gold' and 'Cloth of Gold', but because there is such a difference of description within the correspondence and, in the case of Carter's, an even greater difference to the original description of 1880, we assume that this variety does not now survive. We feel, therefore, that this name could not rightly be applied to a fine variety of double sulphur to-day. Maybe the original Cloth of Gold still survives.

LARGE SULPHUR. (1874, *Villa Gardener*). 'Paler, larger, later than the Early Sulphur.'

YELLOW. (1884, *Gardener's Chronicle*). 'Not sulphur, which has smooth glossy foliage and pale creamy flowers. This yellow has large dented leaves and the flowers are very fine.'

It is hard to say just how many of these eight varieties were, in fact, the same, although differently named. Alex Dean, writing in the *Florist and Pomologist* (1874) of the Giant and Giantess, says they were 'received from Ireland, so named'. The editor of the 'In the Garden' feature in the *Journal of Horticulture* of 1885 writes, 'Take the sulphurs and yellows for example. There is the early and late sulphur, the latter being the largest and rather deeper in colour and I do not distinguish between it and what is sold as Giant and Giantess. I have dropped these names. Cloth of Gold is a rich lemon yellow, very double and rather late and quite distinct from the rest.'

In distinguishing one variety from another, the flowers themselves may well prove to be the most unreliable feature. It is clear that the exact colour of any flower undergoes considerable change from the moment when it first opens to that stage just before it withers. In the case of the double sulphur primroses, what may start as pale sulphur may end as yellow. But the difference in the shape of the buds, the colour and degree of hairiness of leaves, are important features. And we believe that the criterion of merit depends very largely on the shape of the flower. If it is a neat, well-formed rosette of petals, then it is a good variety. On the other hand, many double sulphur primroses seem to open on one side of the bud first, giving a badly-shaped flower. Lastly, the flower should be carried on a stalk sufficiently strong to hold the flower well out from the leaves. A variety that has elegant flowers, well carried on long stems above dark green leaves, even if it is not noticeably free-flowering, is a more attractive plant than one which is covered with ill-shaped flowers, so profusely produced that they support themselves.

To judge from our own correspondence we suppose that there are some fine varieties in existence. The writers say, for example, that they have plants in their gardens which they have always known since they were children and then they ask for their names. We hope that we have made it sufficiently clear that the names, in themselves, are unimportant and that it is only the quality of the particular variety that really matters, for there must be dozens of varieties of doubles hidden in the borders of cottage gardens, many of them more lovely and unique than those listed by us here.

To conclude our work on double primroses, may we add that recognition by the Royal Horticultural Society of very many of the varieties (also of the *Juliae* hybrids) is long overdue. It is unthinkable that such established varieties as Red Paddy, Our Pat, Tyrian Purple, Bon Accord Elegans and others should have as yet received no official recognition. It should be realized by those in authority that the primrose in all its forms is now enjoying the utmost popularity with the modern Elizabethan gardener, so that these charming, hardy and useful plants should no longer be kept in the background by those who do not know them.

CHAPTER XI

The Auriculas

It is quite unthinkable to write a book on primroses and polyanthus without just one chapter on the auricula, for the three subjects go hand in hand, the correct title of the Auricula Society being the National Auricula and Primula Society. Most primrose lovers try their hand with the garden auriculas but leave the show varieties to experienced specialist growers, for they are the 'malmaisons' of the primrose world. They must be flowered under glass in pots and be given a reasonably sulphur-free atmosphere; the alpine and garden varieties can be grown successfully under much the same conditions as the single and double primroses. The alpine auricula was introduced to England by the Flemish weavers who took refuge here about the year 1580. The plant was first described by Gerard in 1597 and at the beginning of the seventeenth century Parkinson, in his *Theatre of Plants*, named twenty-five varieties, giving them the more unfamiliar name of 'Beares Ears', by which they were then known. By 1665, John Rea gives us a most detailed account of the plant in his *Flora*, for by that date named varieties were being constantly introduced. It was the north-west Midland corner of England that first became the centre of the auricula enthusiasts, the counties of Cheshire, Lancashire and north Staffordshire, and to this day this part of England has remained the focal point of the auricula.

It was during the early seventeenth century that the plant enjoyed its greatest popularity both in Britain and on the Continent; indeed, in many of the paintings of flower groups by Dutch artists of the seventeenth century, the auricula receives prominence and is generally shown in the pale grey or brown forms, the 'tawny, ash, haire and dun' colours given us in Hanmer's *Garden Book*. Three hundred years ago, the double and striped forms were common, but their popularity waned before the more refined reds, blues and yellows as the years went by; and to-day the original forms appear to be almost extinct.

Originating in the Alps, the alpine and garden auriculas became established in England, for they were easy to cultivate; and with the polyanthus as we know it, and the *Juliae* primroses then unknown, they became greatly esteemed plants for early summer flowering. By the middle of the eighteenth century, named varieties having green and white edges became known, and were the forerunners of our modern exhibition auriculas.

One of the great differences between the alpine and show auriculas is revealed in the 'paste' or 'meal' which appears on both foliage and bloom. All types, except the green-edged varieties, carry meal on their leaves. This is, in fact, a covering of minute glandular hairs which increase the silvery appearance of the foliage as their density increases.

About the middle of the eighteenth century there occurred an amazing change in the make-up of a number of auricula flowers. For the first time it was observed that the edges of various varieties were either green, grey or white, the same characteristics causing this as were causing the mealiness of the foliage, the white being so densely covered with microscopic hairs that it had the appearance of a white 'paste'. The result of this was actually the replacement of the petals by structures identical with that of the leaves. The appearance of this 'paste' led to the cultivation, primarily for exhibition purposes, of those auriculas possessing this strange feature, for now some form of protection was needed to preserve the 'paste' from damage by rain. By the year 1800 the show auricula had raced away from its alpine relation in point of popularity, as seventeen requirements to satisfy the judges had been determined and the nurseryman's catalogues listed at least a hundred varieties!

For show purposes the auricula of the exhibition bench must be one of four distinct types.

a. The Green-Edge, having a pure green edge quite free of meal, but with the paste in the centre quite smooth and perfectly round.

b. The Grey-Edge, which have a slight sprinkling of meal over the green edge, giving the edge a grey-like appearance.

c. The White-Edge, which is completely covered with meal or *farina* and generally with the body a very pure dark colour, the effect of which is most striking.

d. The self-coloured show varieties, which have the same white paste centre but no green tissue on the edge of the petals.

The alpine auricula, the originator of the show types, contains no meal either in the centre or on the petals. The centre is generally gold in colour, the body being dark, shading to a lighter colour at the edges of the petals.

Shade is perhaps the most important consideration when growing the show auricula under glass or the alpine varieties in the open ground. A north aspect is ideal for border or glass, or behind a high wall where the plants will receive some shade from the sun during the mid-summer months. The alpines may be cultivated in any situation in any part of the British Isles for they are completely hardy, and being used to outdoor treatment for several hundred years, no amount of adverse weather conditions will cause serious damage, unless it be excessive moisture.

Alpine auriculas enjoy a deeply cultivated loamy soil in which has been incorporated a liberal dressing of bone meal. The ground should be well drained, for stagnant water will cause rotting of the thick rootstock. Planting is best done late in August when the weather and soil conditions are generally suitable and the plants have had time to produce offsets large enough to handle. It must here be said that because the alpine auricula does not carry any of the strange 'meal' that appears on the show types, it is not equally prized on the show bench. Of more recent years it has been the tendency to make almost every variety a 'pot' plant, which has done nothing to help to maintain the sturdy constitution of the alpine varieties. It is suggested that where it is possible to grow one or two of each variety in the open ground, this should be done, for though the auricula takes reasonably kindly to restricted pot conditions, it thrives even better in a border with unrestricted root run. Where possible, stock plants for propagation purposes should be confined to a border, and the offsets introduced to the pots when required. The show varieties may also be kept quite free from disease if allowed to occupy some time in the border, and especially should the stock plants be grown in this way.

During very severe winter weather some protection may be given. The offsets for growing on for show purposes should be removed from the plants late in August, half the number being potted and the rest re-planted in the border. Firm planting into a prepared bed should be given to those being planted outside, but otherwise no special preparation of the soil will be necessary. But the compost for the pots throughout the growing period of the show auricula has for years been the subject of diverse opinion; almost every grower seems to have his own methods. To-day, however, nearly every grower makes use of the almost sterile peat mosses, for a compost rich in peat will ensure a healthy, vigorous rooting system and will retain moisture in the pots to a considerable degree.

For seedling plants, Mrs. Florence Levy recommends this mixture; to three bushels of good loam, add the same amount of coarse sand, then add two bushels of granulated peat and a like amount of a Canadian preparation called 'Blue Whale', which is dried sphagnum moss with a soluble whale preparation incorporated to provide a steady supply of food value. In Britain bone meal or flour appears to give the same result as the whale preparation, but many large growers fight shy of this fertilizer, for it has a tendency to produce harmful maggots in the soil. At the nurseries of Mr. James Douglas at Edenside, one of the largest growers of auriculas in England, the compost used consists of four parts of fibrous loam which is put through a half-inch sieve, one part of well-rotted manure, and one part of leaf mould; and to the whole is mixed a small quantity of sharp sand. In place of sand some enthusiasts use powdered charcoal, for this not only keeps the compost 'open' in texture, it has the additional power of absorbing the carbonic acid and ammonia from the atmosphere, which are an additional source of nourishment for the plants. Also, being black in colour, it provides additional warmth to the compost.

Many growers use the John Innes Compost, the formula of which is:

> 7 parts sterilized loam
> 3 parts granulated peat
> 2 parts coarse sand

to each bushel of which is added:

> ¾ oz. ground chalk or limestone
> ¼ lb. John Innes Base Compost

Many substitute for the Base 1 oz. of superphosphate, and this is said to give excellent results.

When re-potting both alpine and show auriculas and also double primroses the old soil, which may contain woolly aphis, should be discarded entirely and the old plants should first have their rootstock washed quite free of the old soil in a solution of carbolic soap. All old plants of auriculas should, in addition, have their roots dipped in methylated spirits as a secondary precaution against aphis. Old plant pots should also be subjected to the same treatment before re-potting takes place. It is necessary, too, to inspect the 'carrot' portion of the root and cut away any parts that may have become decayed. All off-sets will be removed and re-potted at the same time as the parent plant. Then comes the important procedure of watering.

Neither the show nor alpine auricula (and this applies also to the double primrose) will tolerate too much water, especially until the plants are thoroughly re-established, and this care in watering must apply to seedlings too. Over-watering, particularly at the start, will cause nothing but trouble. Keep the compost just moist and shield the plants from any strong sunshine. The plants will continue to make headway until late November, when they begin to reach a dormant stage, and remain thus until March. They may then be given more water to bring the plants on into bloom. All types of auriculas are quite hardy and should need nothing more than a frame to afford them protection from winter rains. Excess damp will cause trouble if the plants are allowed to remain in the open. When April arrives and the buds are forming, the greatest care must be given to the plants so that the blooms reach perfection as a culminating point of one's labours. Watering and shading must go hand in hand, for any carelessness in these essential procedures may cause the paste on the bloom to be completely spoilt. Show auriculas are such strange plants that those that may be had in bloom must not be subjected to any unorthodox treatment, as spoiling is all too easy. Some varieties flower only at intervals, others bloom well over a period of years and then give up the game completely. Certain varieties may produce only a few blooms one year, yet in the following year may be a glorious mass of colour. There is no knowing exactly just what they will do, so it pays to give the satisfactory plant the utmost care when the bloom is opening.

Auriculas may be grown from seed, but do not germinate very easily. Indeed a box sown with seed should never be discarded until at least twelve months have elapsed from the sowing date, for seed is expensive to buy and the finest plants may come from seeds that may be the last to germinate.

An ideal seed sowing compost consists of well-sieved Kettering loam to which has been added a liberal amount of granulated peat and an equal quantity of coarse sand. The peat must first be subjected to heavy watering so as to have it in a moist condition before mixing into the compost. Peat will ensure a heavy root run of the tiny seedlings and will also conserve moisture and reduce watering to a minimum while germination is taking place.

Seed should be sown as soon as it is ripe, generally about the first of July, and the plants will flower for the first time in twenty months. The seed should be pressed into the compost when sown, but should not be covered with soil. After gentle watering, a sheet of clean glass should be placed over the box or pan, which is placed in a greenhouse or closed frame. The first seedlings may show in a few weeks, but it is generally those that are more stubborn to germinate which produce the finest bloom.

It is not suggested that this short chapter on auriculas is at all comprehensive. It is said that the growers of the north-west Midlands have spent a lifetime on the study of the show auricula, and the beginner should feel his way. The alpine types should offer no trouble, and for ordinary purposes may be cultivated alongside the single and double primroses and polyanthus. After all they are members of the same family and their inclusion in the primrose garden will create added interest. To quote Mr. Dan Bamford, of Middleton in Lancashire, in the 1950 Year Book of the National Auricula and Primula Society: 'The alpine auricula is a very different proposition. It is easier to grow and we ought to have far more growers in this Section.' Priced at between three and five shillings each, the alpines are inexpensive as well as hardy. Of the fifty or so varieties known to the authors, all are easy to cultivate, highly colourful, and ideal subjects for the rockery or border in late spring. They will extend the primrose season and give enhanced interest during those exciting spring months.

Growers who may wish to take up the cultivation of these delightful plants on a larger scale would be well advised to purchase the late Sir Rowland Biffen's great work, *The Auricula*, published by the Cambridge University Press. It is the most comprehensive work on this plant ever to appear.

A few easy and popular varieties for the beginner in both the show and alpine sections are listed below.

SHOW VARIETIES

Green Edge

DONALD HAYSOM. This is generally offered at two guineas a plant but is a new variety and a superb introduction.

COPYTHORNE. Another new variety, and like the above is likely to supersede many of the older 'greens'.

CULVERLEY. A grand variety that has received an Award of Merit.

ANTONIO. An older green but easy to grow and is recommended to the beginner.

White Edge

HINTON ADMIRAL. This grand variety was chosen first of its class at the 1952 Show of the Southern Section of the Auricula Society.

WILVERLEY. One of the most popular of the white-edged varieties.

ACME. An easy variety and still most popular on the show bench.

Grey Edge

SOMERLEY. A new 'grey' possessing a good tube and refined body colour and likely to become the most popular of the section.

SHERFIELD. Another lovely grey which has received an Award of Merit.

SWAY. Like the two previous varieties this was raised by C. G. Haysom of Southampton, which is sufficient recommendation.

NUTHATCH. The easiest and one of the most popular of all the 'greys'.

Selfs

HARRISON WEIR. Without doubt the most striking self with its deep scarlet blooms of perfect form. Mr. Dan Bamford, that great authority on the show auricula, says, 'I know of no recent variety to replace it'.

ALICE HAYSOM. Another fine bright crimson that is becoming more popular every year.

ROSEBUD. This is a delightful and unusual rose-pink self of easy growth.

BLUE FIRE. This should be in every beginner's collection for its ease of cultivation and its delightful pure bright blue colours.

ALPINE AURICULAS

White Centre

ARGUS. A grand beginner's variety of excellent habit. The body colour is rich plum.

ANNE CRISP. An attractive bright purple, shaded magenta.

BLUE BONNET. Rich violet-blue shading to mid-blue, very lovely.

FAWLEY. Of intense violet-blue shaded lighter blue.

JOY. A newer variety of rich velvet crimson.

Gold Centre

AFRICAN CHIEF. A most striking variety of deep maroon shading to bright crimson.

BOOKHAM FIREFLY. The above variety but in reverse and equally attractive.

CAROLINA. Possesses a superb gold centre and its colouring is most unusual; the rich crimson is shaded to apricot.

GOLDEN CHALICE. Has a perfect centre and a body colour of rich golden-bronze.

KINGCUP. Of rich, bright crimson shaded brown, this is perhaps the finest of the alpines, having a gold centre.

GORDON DOUGLAS. An old favourite, having a centre of a rich cream colour and the body a deep violet-purple.

MRS. FLORENCE LEVY. A most striking alpine. The body of the petals is black, ringed with scarlet and edged apricot-orange.

MIDAS. A popular and easily grown old favourite, being of a rich velvet-brown colour, shaded golden bronze.

PRINCE JOHN. A very richly coloured bloom of deep crimson shading to deep maroon.

THE GARDEN AURICULA

While the show and alpine varieties were introduced to Britain from our near European neighbours, and are cultivated chiefly by specialist growers, there is a race of auriculas that were here long before the continental varieties reached our island four hundred years ago. Because there are so many lovely varieties in the premier section, our own native plant has received little attention from the specialist auricula growers, indeed the plant is in much the same form as it was known to Tudor gardeners. And yet it is not only a most charming flower, but is most useful in the primrose garden. Indeed, to the true primrose lover, this section has much to offer, and a selection of plants should be incorporated in every collection. Their great value lies in their ability to withstand a dry soil and one which may be considered relatively impoverished. In the

Miniature Polyanthus: var. Fair Maid

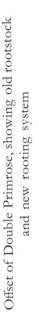

Offset of Double Primrose, showing old rootstock
and new rooting system

town garden they are indispensable as a spring flowering plant, being valuable when planted in those out-of-the-way corners which abound in town gardens. To the front of the shrubbery, and beneath a high wall where the soil is generally of an acid nature (having for years received deposits of soot and quantities of ivy leaves), the old garden auriculas will put up a brave show. They are also charming when used as an edging to a path or lawn. They are extremely hardy and vigorous growers and have an additional value in that they come into flower at a time when the first flush of primrose bloom is finishing. They are at their best during May.

These old-fashioned auriculas readily form offsets and are very easy to divide and re-establish, but though they will thrive in almost any soil provided it is not of a heavy, wet nature, they will exceed all expectation if provided with a little decayed manure and some leaf mould in the soil. An annual dusting with powdered charcoal will considerably help to keep sweet all town soils, and equally useful are an occasional dusting with lime or the forking of limestone rubble into the soil.

Our native garden auricula is known as the old Dusty Miller Auricula, taking its name from the mealy covering of the leaves. There are numerous forms of this group, but one of the most beautiful is a rich wine-red variety, the colour being enhanced by a broad glistening white central ring. There is also a lemon-yellow self of great charm; a navy blue which has the white ring; and many other unique colour variations. Others, less well known and of great charm are the large, sweetly scented Broadwell Gold, the rich scarlet, Southport, and the old purple double flowered, The Bishop. Another lovely variety is Jean Walker, which bears a bloom of pale lavender and has an attractive cream centre. Craig Nordie has coppery-red flowers and unusual grey foilage; and McWatt's Blue, raised by the late Dr. McWatt is a deep navy blue with a conspicuous white eye and is heavily powdered like a show auricula. There are about thirty varieties known to the authors, the collection being well worth having in the garden.

CHAPTER XII

On Showing Primroses and Auriculas

Of all present-day societies devoted to a single flower or genus, that concerned with the auricula is by far the oldest; and to-day the three sections of the National Auricula and Primula Society flourish more vigorously than ever, with a membership drawn from all parts of the world. Every spring, each section holds its own show, which not only enables members and the general public to view both old and new varieties, but also provides a meeting place where members may discuss the respective merit of the various plants.

There are also other shows where polyanthus, primroses and auriculas may be exhibited by both amateur and professional growers, from the *Daily Mail* Ideal Home Exhibition in March, to the Chelsea Show which is held towards the end of May. Prize money is awarded for as many as up to forty classes.

At the Show held by the Northern Section of the Society a list of four Sections will provide the novice grower with at least one or two classes in which to compete. For all those who are interested in these lovely plants, it is pleasant to know that there is at least something for every taste. As a matter of additional interest the various named varieties of the winning entries are given by kind permission of the Society. At random, the details of the 1951 Show have been chosen:

SECTION I

Class 1—*Six Show Auriculas* (four dissimilar).

    1. F. Buckley   Scarlet Prince; Nuthatch; Sherfield; Culverley; Dilton Gray; Mikado

Class 2—*Four Show Auriculas* (dissimilar).

    1. T. Meek   Shadow; Geo. Rudd; Clouded Yellow; Capt. Hearn

Class 3—*Three Show Auriculas* (dissimilar).
    1. W. Riddle   Patriot; Sloden; Sherfield
Class 4—*Two Show Auriculas* (dissimilar).
    1. R. Loake   Sway; J. W. Midgeley (Premier)
Class 5—*Two Show Auriculas* (Novice Class).
    No Award
Class 6—*One Show Auricula* (Green Edge).
    1. T. Meek   Tinkerbell
Class 7—*One Show Auricula* (Grey Edge).
    1. R. Loake   Marmion
Class 8—*One Show Auricula* (White Edge).
    1. R. Loake   Harvestslade
Class 9—*One Show Auricula* (Self).
    1. F. Buckley   Harrison Weir
Class 10—*One Show Auricula* (Yellow Self).
    1. Capt. Hearn   Mary Winn
Class 11—*Three Show Auriculas* (Selfs)
    1. T. Meek   Mikado; Martha; Sally
Class 12—*One Show Auricula* (Edged Seedling).
    1. T. Meek   Lime (Green Edge)
Class 13—*One Show Auricula* (Self Seedling).
    No Award
Premier Show Auricula.
    R. Loake with J. W. Midgeley

SECTION II

Class 14—*Six Plants* (four dissimilar).
    1. F. Buckley   Goldfinch; J. W. Gardiner; Gordon
                       Douglas; Joy; Golden Glory; Argus
Class 15—*Four Plants* (dissimilar).
    1. F. Faulkner   Verdi; Lady Daresbury; Joy; Seedling
Class 16—*Three Plants* (dissimilar).
    1. Dr. Hough   Gordon Douglas; Bratley; F. Crosland
Class 17—*Two Plants* (dissimilar).
    1. J. Bamford   Gordon Douglas; Doris

Class 18—*Two Plants* (Novice Class).
    1. C. H. Griffiths   Winsor; Majestic
Class 19—*One Plant* (Gold-centred).
    1. Mrs. Hough   Golden Glory
Class 20—*One Plant* (Light-centred).
    1. F. Faulkner   Joy (Premier)
Class 21—*One Plant* (Alpine Seedling).
    1. F. Faulkner   Frank Faulkner
Premier Alpine Auricula.
    F. Faulkner, with Joy

SECTION III

Class 22—*Pair Primroses.*
    1. Capt. Hawkes   Grace Eddolls; Mina Ellis
Class 23—*Pair Double Primroses.*
    1. Mrs. Hawkes   Bon Accord Cerise; Bon Accord Lilac
Class 24—*Pair Garden Polyanthus.*
    1. Capt. Hearn
Class 25—*Pair Garden Auriculas.*
    1. F. Woodcock
Class 26—*Pair Juliae Primroses.*
    1. Dr. Newton   Tawny Port; Blue Horizon
Class 27—*Three Primulas* (dissimilar, Novice Class).
    1. A. L. Watkins   Unnamed
Class 28—*One Primula* (any variety).
    1. J. P. Howson   Celtic King
Class 29—*Six Primulas.*
    1. H. Brierley   Faldonside; (2) Frondosa; Celtic King;
                                Hirsuta Alba (2)

SECTION IV
POLYANTHUS, GOLD-LACED

Class 31—*One Red Ground.*
    1. Dr. Hough
Class 32—*One Black Ground.*
    1. J. Antrobus

Class 33—*One Each Red and Black.*

   1. J. Antrobus

Class 34—*One Seedling* (any colour).

   1. J. Antrobus

Class 35—*One Pan or Bowl* (any plant in primula families).

   1. J. P. Howson

There were four hundred and fifty entries altogether, fairly evenly divided among the first three sections, the gold-laced polyanthus (Section IV) being now only lightly represented, though there is now a revival of interest in these lovely old-world plants.

The present society was re-formed in 1872 and in that year held its first show under its new title in Manchester, with the Rev. F. D. Horner as secretary. It is interesting to note that there were just seven classes represented, all show and alpine auriculas, with one class for single plants of polyanthus—single and double primroses were still only in the remote cottage gardens, slowly passing out of existence until the Cocker Brothers revived interest in them at the beginning of the twentieth century; and though it was decided to inaugurate a class for 'twelve single and double primroses' in 1878, this was abolished fifteen years later, possibly on account of lack of entries or interest in the plants. Through the years the polyanthus, especially the gold-laced varieties, held their place in the affections of enthusiasts, but it was not until 1947 that classes for primroses were again included in the schedule.

Now let us look at some of the rules and regulations imposed by the show judges. First the auricula. In all classes, one truss only must be left on each plant, and the leaves should be such that they will cover the soil in the pots. Show and alpine auriculas and gold-laced polyanthus must be shown with not less than five expanded pips, and with auriculas this has of recent years been taken to mean five and only five pips. The ideal show auricula should be carried on a strong stem and must have the individual blooms balanced round the stem so that they have sufficient room to display their complete proportions. The blooms should be quite round, with completely smooth edges, and be flat when fully opened. The mouth of the tube of the flower should be of a lemon-yellow colour. The paste should be circular, its diameter one-half the size of the bloom. The edge of course determines the class in which the auricula is shown.

The chief faults to-day seem to be too much ground colour which runs on to the edges, in parts completely spoiling the bloom. Another fault is that the petals do not overlap, and thereby the flower loses its neat, flat appearance.

Pointed petals will also earn adverse points, as will weak and irregular body colour.

With gold-laced polyanthus, each pip (or bloom) should be flat and as near circular as possible. Also, the width of the centre and the body colour should be the same. Most important is the lacing; this should be in proportion to the size of the individual pip.

Neat stakes may be used to support the stems of auriculas and polyanthus, but packing between the individual blooms is not allowed on the show bench.

When showing single and double primroses, the main consideration is the quantity and general quality of the bloom, for here no rules are set down as to formation of the bloom. Thin wire supports may be used for those varieties having a polyanthus stem, such as Fair Maid and Lady Greer.

As with all auriculas and primroses, the quality or condition of the bloom when presented will be the determining factor. All bloom which is not up to standard should be carefully removed at the base, also any leaves ruined by slugs or having 'brown edge'. In the auricula and the polyanthus any badly formed pips must also be removed, the exhibitor bearing in mind that at least five pips must remain to satisfy the judges; more than five should be present if possible. These points all may attend to; it is the correct timing of the presentation of the plants in every section that calls for experience and the utmost care. A sunny spring will mean that watering will demand the greatest attention and the combination of sunshine and water can bring the blooms to maturity several weeks before the date of the show. Damping down of the greenhouse or frame and careful shading will do much to defer the opening of the blooms. Where single and double primroses are being grown in the open ground, specimen plants should be potted into 60-size pots early in March, lifting as much soil with the roots as possible so as not to cause undue disturbance.

With primroses, early flowering varieties will, of course, be brought on for early shows by covering the plants with frames or cloches. The show season may be greatly extended by careful shading of the later-flowering plants. Presentation and naming will be just as important as care of the plant, and one sees so many otherwise excellent plants spoilt by slackness in final presentation.

On show day, the pots should be washed quite clean; and where possible, do use an earthenware pot of new appearance. The compost should be covered either with small limestone chippings or fresh moss, though chippings will remain in position better when the plants are moved and also tend to show the plants off to better advantage. Naming is important, a square card size about 1½ inches by 1 inch being ideal, and this should be held up on thin wire or a stick. Make quite sure, if you have to travel some distance, that you will arrive at the place of exhibition in ample time to attend to the final titivating of the plants, for this might make all the difference between first and second prize.

CHAPTER XIII

Pests and Diseases of Primrose and Auricula

So few troubles seem to worry members of the primrose family that to all intents and purposes they may be considered immune; indeed it is rare for either pest or disease to cause trouble in the amateur's collections, though where the plants are grown on a large scale, the usual precautions should be taken to ensure a completely clean stock. The amateur, then, should take care to purchase his plants from a reliable source and he need then worry little about his plants provided they are given the cultural conditions they demand.

Pests

WHITE PRIMROSE APHIS. When the foliage of a primrose plant appears to be turning a sickly yellow colour at a period of the year when the lush deep green colour should predominate, then suspect the white aphis which is perhaps the most common of the very few primula pests. Decayed vegetation may encourage the trouble, so all dead leaves should be constantly removed from the plants.

The white aphis may be found clustered at the base of a plant or even round the roots. A suggested treatment is to lift the plant and to wash off all soil particles before rubbing methylated spirit into the roots and crown. A more modern method, and perhaps more reliable, is to dust Gammexane round the plant and slightly fork this into the soil. Yet another method is to use a diluted solution of nicotine and soft soap, not forgetting that nicotine is poisonous and should be used with care.

GREENFLY. This pest, common to so many garden plants during warm weather, may also infect the primrose leaves; and where a concentration of the pests is observed it will be advisable to take some steps to eradicate them without delay, or the constitution of the plant may be quickly undermined. Spraying with a soft soap solution will prove effective but the applications will need to be repeated over a period. Perhaps a more thorough method would be to lift the plant, wash off most of the soil, and give both foliage and roots a washing in a soft soap solution.

RED SPIDER. Attacks are rarely experienced except following an extreme drought, when it may not be possible to water the plants artificially. If a mulch has been given, this should enable the plants to retain a certain amount of moisture which will ward off red-spider attacks; and where the plants are given the cultural treatment they require, little trouble should be experienced.

SLUGS. During a particularly wet period, when the new season's growth is succulent and attractive to slugs, the pests may easily devour several plants in a night, possibly the choicest of one's collection. Slugs also attack seedlings of polyanthus when these are in the open ground, and even when sown in frames, and may wipe out the product of several pounds' worth of seed in a few hours. A solid form of methylated spirit crushed and mixed with bran and placed six inches from the plants or seedlings will quickly exterminate all slugs over a considerable radius. The bait should be kept away from children and animals; this is not a difficult matter if it is placed in frames or under cloches.

WEEVILS. Root or vine weevils, as they are called, must be taken more seriously than any other pest. Frequently, the half-inch-long, dark grey grubs are found beneath large clumps of hardy primroses and in pot-grown auriculas of both the exhibition and alpine varieties. The pest seems to be more numerous in the south than in the Midlands and north and it is the experience of the authors that though the single and double primroses are rarely attacked, pot and open ground auriculas may suffer greatly. The grubs feed on the roots, which in the auricula are succulent, and considerable damage can be done by a single grub. Their presence may be observed by the sickly appearance of a plant, generally in early spring when the foliage should take on a fresh, rich colour. The presence of weevil larvae in the soil may be noticed by the plant failing to respond to spring conditions in the normal way. First they attack the fibrous roots, then the thick stumpy root, until soon nothing remains below soil level and the plant quickly perishes.

If a plant is removed from the soil, the larvae will generally be seen clustered about the roots or trunk where new growth may be seen to appear. Whereas the greenfly will infect the parts of the plant above soil level, the woolly or root aphis attacks below ground, sucking the sap from all portions of the plant which may be under soil level. This not only greatly undermines the constitution of a plant, but also paves the way for infestation by harmful fungus spores, always ready to attack a weakened plant. Any apparent disease should be cut away with a sharp knife, and the portion of the root where the cut is made should be rubbed with powdered charcoal before the plant is re-potted. Treatment of a plant attacked by weevils will depend upon the seriousness of the attack, for should this be in a too advanced stage, there is little to be done but to burn both plant and soil. The application of methylated spirit to the attacked root or crown of primrose or auricula will exterminate the grubs, but in this case the plant will have to be removed from the soil.

Even if the plant is saved, the re-potting at a time when it should be reaching flowering perfection will bring nothing but disappointment. Far better will it be to follow a programme of prevention. For this we would suggest that the compost for all potted primroses and auriculas be given a very small dusting of Gammexane before planting takes place. A too heavy application has been known to stunt root growth. Miss E. Wilson of Sheffield, an authority on primroses and auriculas, states in the 1952 Year Book of the National Primula Society that she dusts the pots with Gammexane before adding the soil, and also the beds of soil of ashes on which the pots stand in greenhouse or frame, and has noted excellent results. Before planting alpine auriculas, or any of the *Juliae* type primroses and doubles in the border, a slight dusting with this preparation can do nothing but give a measure of control against aphis attack.

WIREWORM. Among primrose and auricula growers, controversy rages as to the harm done by wireworm to the roots of pot and open ground plants. One old grower of repute swears that this pest does absolutely no damage and should be ignored, but once, when lifting and clearing an old border of shrubs and plants, I found a primrose hybridist root in a decayed state, and a number of wireworms were shaken out. Primroses rarely suffer, as we have emphasized, from attacks by pests or disease, and only where wireworms might be found in any quantity need there be fear of damage. In soil where this pest is likely to abound it may be useful to sow a few patches of wheat seed in obtrusive places, just as do dahlia and strawberry growers. Wheat attracts the wireworms, and periodically the germinated seed may be dug up and burnt.

Diseases

ROOT ROT. This trouble may occur where the roots and crowns are exposed to too large amounts of water. Several varieties should be afforded protection from winter rains and excess moisture by planting on the rockery in the crevice of an overhanging stone. Even the *Juliae* varieties and the hose-in-hose section, much as they enjoy a moist soil, resent one which is not well-drained, for in such a soil the fibrous roots will rot.

VIRUS. As with fruit trees, little is known of the cause, though it is apparent that insects such as weevils act as carriers, and greatly undermine the constitution of a plant, making it susceptible to attack from virus and fungus diseases. Yellowing or blotching of the leaves may denote the presence of virus trouble. The plants should be dug up, washed free of all soil particles, and after treating for aphis as described on page 136, the plant should be planted in fresh soil. If the plant fails to recover in a short time, virus may be suspected, and the plant should be destroyed. All plants showing appearance of any trouble should be isolated at once.

Index